WeightWatchers®

Fantastic recipes for every occasion

Fresh & Fabulous

First published in Great Britain by Simon & Schuster UK Ltd, 2013
A CBS Company

Copyright © 2013, Weight Watchers International, Inc.
Simon & Schuster Illustrated Books, Simon & Schuster UK Ltd,
First Floor, 222 Gray's Inn Road, London WC1X 8HB

www.simonandschuster.co.uk

Simon & Schuster Australia, Sydney
Simon & Schuster India, New Delhi

Weight Watchers, **ProPoints** and the **ProPoints** icon are the registered
trademarks of Weight Watchers International Inc and are used under license
by Weight Watchers (UK) Ltd.

Weight Watchers Publications: Jane Griffiths, Linda Palmer and Nina McKerlie.

Recipes written by: Sue Ashworth, Sue Beveridge, Tamsin Burnett-Hall,
Cas Clarke, Siân Davies, Roz Denny, Nicola Graimes, Becky Johnson,
Kim Morphew, Joy Skipper, Penny Stephens and Wendy Veale as well
as Weight Watchers Leaders and Members.

Photography by: Iain Bagwell, Steve Baxter, Steve Lee, Juliet Piddington
and William Shaw.
Project editor: Nicki Lampon.
Design and typesetting: Martin Lampon.

Colour reproduction by Dot Gradations Ltd, UK.
Printed and bound in China.

A CIP catalogue for this book is available from the British Library

ISBN 978-1-47111-091-7

1 2 3 4 5 6 7 8 9 10

Pictured on the title page: Tangy chicken bruschetta p26.
Pictured on the Introduction: Roasted butternut squash and feta salad p22, Citrus
pork steaks with potato salad p70, Balsamic roasted red onion pizza with feta p130.

WeightWatchers®

Fantastic recipes for every occasion

Fresh & Fabulous

SIMON &
SCHUSTER
ILLUSTRATED

London · New York · Sydney · Toronto · New Delhi

A CBS COMPANY

Weight Watchers **ProPoints** Weight Loss System is a simple way to lose weight. As part of the Weight Watchers **ProPoints** plan you'll enjoy eating delicious, healthy, filling foods that help to keep you feeling satisfied for longer and in control of your portions.

Ⓥ This symbol denotes a vegetarian recipe and assumes that, where relevant, free range eggs, vegetarian cheese, vegetarian virtually fat free fromage frais, vegetarian low fat crème fraîche and vegetarian low fat yogurts are used. Virtually fat free fromage frais, low fat crème fraîche and low fat yogurts may contain traces of gelatine so they are not always vegetarian. Please check the labels.

❋ This symbol denotes a dish that can be frozen. Unless otherwise stated, you can freeze the finished dish for up to 3 months. Defrost thoroughly and reheat until the dish is piping hot throughout.

Recipe notes

Egg size: Medium sized, unless otherwise stated.

Raw eggs: Only the freshest eggs should be used. Pregnant women, the elderly and children should avoid recipes with eggs that are not fully cooked or raw.

All fruits and vegetables: Medium sized, unless otherwise stated.

Stock: Stock cubes are used in recipes, unless otherwise stated. These should be prepared according to packet instructions.

Recipe timings: These are approximate and meant to be guidelines. Please note that the preparation time includes all the steps up to and following the main cooking time(s).

Microwaves: Timings and temperatures are for a standard 800 W microwave. If necessary, adjust your own microwave.

Low fat spread: Where a recipe states to use a low fat spread, a light spread with a fat content of no less than 38% should be used.

Low fat soft cheese: Where low fat soft cheese is specified in a recipe, this refers to soft cheese with a fat content of less than 5%.

Contents

Introduction

One of the joys of cooking your own meals is using produce that is *Fresh & Fabulous*, whether it be seasonal fruit and vegetables or fresh, local meat and fish. This wonderful book is packed full of recipes from the best of Weight Watchers cookbooks to help you cook up fantatstic meals that are full of flavour.

Make the most of summer ingredients with Prawns with Lime and Chillies, Chargrilled Vegetable Tabbouleh or Fig and Raspberry Clafoutis. Brighten up winter with a Hearty Turkey Casserole, Balsamic Roasted Red Onion Pizza with Feta or Cream Hearts with Passion Fruit. Whatever your fresh ingredients, or whatever the occasion, there is sure to be a recipe here that suits your needs and is perfect for your family and friends. So get cooking with *Fresh & Fabulous* and show everyone what good food should really taste like.

About Weight Watchers

For more than 40 years Weight Watchers has been helping people around the world to lose weight using a long term sustainable approach. Weight Watchers successful weight loss system is based on four tried and trusted principles:

- Eating healthily
- Being more active
- Adjusting behaviour to help weight loss
- Getting support in weekly meetings

Our unique ***ProPoints*** system empowers you to manage your food plan and make wise recipe choices for a healthier, happier you.

To find out more about Weight Watchers and the ***ProPoints*** values for these recipes contact Customer Service on 0845 345 1500.

Storing and freezing

Making meals ahead of time and storing and freezing them is one of the keys to producing healthy tasty meals during a busy week. Many dishes store well in the fridge, but make sure you use them up within a day or two. Some can also be frozen. Try making double the quantity when you cook a recipe and storing the extra portions in the freezer. This way you'll always have a fantastic selection of meals that you can pull out and reheat at the end of a busy day. However, it is important to make sure you know how to freeze safely.

- Wrap any food to be frozen in rigid containers or strong freezer bags. This is important to stop foods contaminating each other or getting freezer burn.
- Label the containers or bags with the contents and date – your freezer should have a star marking that tells you how long you can keep different types of frozen food.
- Never freeze warm food – always let it cool completely first.
- Never freeze food that has already been frozen and defrosted.
- Freeze food in portions, then you can take out as little or as much as you need each time.
- Defrost what you need in the fridge, making sure you put anything that might have juices, such as meat, on a covered plate or in a container.
- Fresh food, such as raw meat and fish, should be wrapped and frozen as soon as possible.
- Most fruit and vegetables can be frozen by open freezing. Lay them out on a tray, freeze until solid and then pack them into bags.
- Some vegetables, such as peas, broccoli and broad beans, can be blanched first by cooking for 2 minutes in boiling water. Drain, refresh under cold water and then freeze once cold.

- Fresh herbs are great frozen – either seal leaves in bags or, for soft herbs such as basil and parsley, chop finely and add to ice cube trays with water. These are great for dropping into casseroles or soups straight from the freezer.

Some things cannot be frozen. Whole eggs do not freeze well, but yolks and whites can be frozen separately. Vegetables with a high water content, such as salad leaves, celery and cucumber, will not freeze. Fried foods will be soggy if frozen, and sauces such as mayonnaise will separate when thawed and should not be frozen.

Shopping hints and tips

Always buy the best ingredients you can afford. If you are going to cook healthy meals, it is worth investing in some quality ingredients that will really add flavour to your dishes. When buying meat, choose lean cuts of meat or lean mince, and if you are buying precooked sliced meat, buy it fresh from the deli counter.

When you're going around the supermarket it's tempting to pick up foods you like and put them in your trolley without thinking about how you will use them. So, a good plan is to decide what dishes you want to cook before you go shopping, check your store cupboard and make a list of what you need. You'll save time by not drifting aimlessly around the supermarket picking up what you fancy.

We've added a checklist here for some of the storecupboard ingredients used in this book. Just add fresh ingredients in your regular shop and you'll be ready to cook the wonderful recipes in *Fresh & Fabulous*.

Store cupboard checklist

- [ ] almonds, flaked
- [ ] artificial sweetener
- [ ] bay leaves
- [ ] beans, canned
- [ ] breadcrumbs, dried natural
- [ ] bulgur wheat, dried
- [ ] capers, in a jar
- [ ] cayenne pepper
- [ ] chick peas, canned
- [ ] chilli flakes
- [ ] chilli sauce, sweet
- [ ] chocolate, plain
- [ ] cinnamon, ground
- [ ] cooking spray, calorie controlled
- [ ] coriander, ground
- [ ] cornflour
- [ ] couscous, dried
- [ ] cumin (seeds and ground)
- [ ] curry pastes

- [ ] curry powders
- [ ] custard, ready-made
- [ ] fennel seeds
- [ ] fish sauce
- [ ] flour, plain white
- [ ] garam masala
- [ ] herbs, dried
- [ ] honey, clear
- [ ] horseradish sauce
- [ ] lentils, green canned
- [ ] mango chutney
- [ ] mayonnaise, reduced fat
- [ ] mint jelly
- [ ] mustard (Dijon and wholegrain)
- [ ] mustard seeds
- [ ] noodles, dried
- [ ] oil (olive, sunflower and sesame)
- [ ] olives, stoned black in a jar
- [ ] paprika

- [ ] passata
- [ ] pasta, dried
- [ ] peppercorns
- [ ] peppers, in a jar
- [ ] pineapple, canned in natural juice
- [ ] polenta, dried
- [ ] quinoa, dried
- [ ] redcurrant jelly
- [ ] rice, dried
- [ ] saffron strands
- [ ] salt
- [ ] sesame seeds
- [ ] soy sauce
- [ ] sponge fingers
- [ ] stock cubes
- [ ] sugar
- [ ] tomato purée
- [ ] tomatoes, canned
- [ ] vanilla extract
- [ ] vinegars
- [ ] Worcestershire sauce

Light bites

Eggs benedict

Serves 2
259 calories per serving
Takes 15 minutes

1 tablespoon malt vinegar
1 tablespoon Hollandaise
   sauce
2 x 25 g (1 oz) lean bacon
   medallions
1 beef tomato
1 English-style white muffin,
   split in half
2 eggs
½ tablespoon chopped fresh
   parsley, to garnish

Try this tasty variation on bacon and eggs. It's great for weekend guests too.

1 Preheat the grill to medium. Bring a pan of water to a gentle simmer and then add the vinegar. Place two ovenproof plates in the oven and turn to Gas Mark 1/140°C/fan oven 120°C. Spoon the Hollandaise sauce into a small ramekin dish and pop in the oven on the plates to warm through. (If you don't have a separate grill, you can warm the plates by putting them in a bowl of clean hot water until you need them. The sauce heats in seconds in a microwave).

2 Grill the bacon medallions for a minute or two on each side. Cut the beef tomato so that you have two thick slices and grill these until warmed through. Grill the muffin halves until lightly toasted. Top the muffin halves with the bacon and tomato slices and keep them warm on the prepared plates.

3 Meanwhile, break an egg into a cup and then slide it gently into the simmering water. Repeat with the other egg and poach for 4 minutes or until the eggs are cooked to your liking.

4 Remove the eggs from the water with a slotted spoon and place on top of the muffin halves. Top with the warm Hollandaise sauce, sprinkle with the parsley and serve immediately.

Tips... Most supermarkets now do their own smoked bacon medallions. They are simply the leanest part of a bacon rasher with all visible fat removed.

Hollandaise sauce can be difficult to make. However, the ready-made version in jars is excellent.

Baked asparagus and egg tarts

Serves 4
141 calories per serving
Takes 25 minutes

½ a kettleful of boiling water

75 g (2¾ oz) fine asparagus tips

calorie controlled cooking spray

4 x 25 g (1 oz) sheets filo pastry, measuring approximately 24 cm (9½ inches) square

2 teaspoons Dijon mustard

4 eggs

salt and freshly ground black pepper

Serve with a generous side salad, with fat free dressing.

1 Preheat the oven to Gas Mark 5/190°C/fan oven 170°C. Put the boiling water in a saucepan and bring it back to the boil. Add the asparagus tips and cook for 1 minute. Drain and dry with kitchen towel. Set aside.

2 Spray a four hole Yorkshire pudding tin with the cooking spray. Take one sheet of filo pastry and spray with the cooking spray. Fold into quarters to make a 12 cm (4½ inch) square and use to line one hole in the tin. Repeat with the remaining filo sheets. Bake for 5 minutes.

3 Remove the tin from the oven and carefully spread the mustard over the base of each filo case. Divide the asparagus tips equally between the bases and crack an egg into each hole.

4 Season and return to the oven for 10–15 minutes until the egg is just cooked. Serve immediately.

Bacon and egg open ravioli

Serves 2
222 calories per serving
Takes 15 minutes

4 rashers lean back bacon
250 g (9 oz) cherry or vine
tomatoes, on the vine
2 eggs
1 sheet fresh lasagne,
measuring 17 x 22 cm
(6½ x 8½ inches), halved
freshly ground black pepper

This is an unusual take on a cooked breakfast.

1 Preheat the grill to medium. Cook the bacon and tomatoes, vine side down, under the grill for 3–5 minutes until done to your liking. Keep warm.

2 Meanwhile, bring a shallow pan of water to the boil. Break an egg into a cup and then slide it gently into the simmering water. Repeat with the other egg and poach for 4 minutes or until the eggs are cooked to your liking. Remove from the water with a slotted spoon and keep warm.

3 Bring the water back to the boil, add the pasta and cook according to the packet instructions. Drain well and place each sheet on a warm plate. Top each pasta sheet with two rashers of bacon and an egg and loosely fold over to create an open ravioli. Grind over some black pepper and serve the tomatoes on the side.

Lemon chicken and couscous salad

Serves 4

396 calories per serving

Takes 20 minutes + cooling

❄ (for up to 1 month)

250 g (9 oz) dried couscous

300 ml (10 fl oz) hot chicken stock

2 cm (¾ inch) fresh root ginger, grated

1 red pepper, halved and de-seeded

1 yellow pepper, halved and de-seeded

1 courgette, grated

1 small carrot, peeled and grated

1 tablespoon chopped fresh mint

2 tablespoons chopped fresh coriander

grated zest and juice of a lemon

2 x 150 g (5½ oz) cooked skinless chicken breasts, shredded

salt and freshly ground black pepper

75 g (2¾ oz) watercress or salad leaves, to serve

This makes a great summer picnic dish.

1 Preheat the grill to high. Place the couscous in a bowl and pour over the hot stock. Cover with a clean tea towel and leave to soak for 10–15 minutes. Add the grated ginger and stir in with a fork.

2 Meanwhile, place the pepper halves, skin side up, under the grill and cook until very charred. Place in a bowl and cover with cling film until cool enough to handle. Peel off the skin and cut into strips.

3 When the couscous is cool, stir vigorously with a fork and then stir in all the other ingredients, including the pepper strips. Season well and serve on a bed of watercress or salad leaves.

Broad bean and Parma ham salad

Serves 4
140 calories per serving
Takes 15 minutes

450 g (1 lb) shelled fresh or
   frozen broad beans
8 thin slices Parma ham,
   sliced into little strips
juice of ½ a lemon
a small bunch of fresh parsley,
   chopped finely
2 teaspoons olive oil
salt and freshly ground black
   pepper

*A satisfying, bright green salad that is best made with
small, tender broad beans that can be bought fresh or
frozen.*

1 Bring a large pan of water to the boil, add the broad beans
and blanch for 2 minutes. Drain and refresh under cold water.

2 Put the beans in a serving bowl, add all the other
ingredients, toss together and serve.

Variation... Use wafer thin honey roast ham instead of
Parma ham.

Roasted butternut squash and feta salad

Serves 6
191 calories per serving
Takes 15 minutes to prepare,
30 minutes to cook

**700 g (1 lb 9 oz) butternut
squash, peeled, de-seeded
and cut into chunks**

**6 beetroots, peeled and
quartered**

**8 whole garlic cloves,
unpeeled**

**calorie controlled cooking
spray**

1 tablespoon dried chilli flakes

2 tablespoons pumpkin seeds

200 g bag mixed salad leaves

**110 g (4 oz) reduced fat feta
cheese, crumbled**

For the dressing

**2 tablespoons extra virgin
olive oil**

**2 tablespoons balsamic
vinegar**

*A delicious and colourful salad that combines the heat of
chilli and the tang of Greek cheese with the sweetness
of warm roasted vegetables.*

1 Preheat the oven to Gas Mark 6/200°C/fan oven 180°C.
Place the butternut squash, beetroot and garlic in a roasting
tin and spray with the cooking spray. Sprinkle over the chilli
flakes and roast for 30 minutes, turning occasionally, until the
vegetables are softened and charred at the edges.

2 Meanwhile, brown the pumpkin seeds by dry-frying them
in a non stick frying pan, moving them around the pan for
2–3 minutes until they just change colour and begin popping.
Set aside.

3 Remove the squash and beetroot from the oven and leave to
cool slightly. Remove the garlic cloves from the tin.

4 For the dressing, pop the garlic cloves from their skins (they
should slide out easily) and mash the flesh with the olive oil
and vinegar.

5 To serve, arrange the salad leaves on serving plates, top
with the butternut squash and beetroot and crumble over the
feta. Sprinkle over the pumpkin seeds and the salad dressing.

Lamb brochettes with honey and lemon

Serves 4

225 calories per serving

Takes 30 minutes +
  marinating

**400 g (14 oz) lean lamb leg
steaks, trimmed of visible fat
and cut into 8 strips**

**2 lemons, each cut into
quarters**

**1 tablespoon clear honey,
heated**

For the marinade

**150 g (5 oz) low fat natural
yogurt**

4 garlic cloves, crushed

**a small bunch of fresh mint,
chopped**

**salt and freshly ground black
pepper**

*Serve in a medium pitta bread or with 60 g (2 oz) dried rice
per person, cooked according to the packet instructions.*

1 Thread the lamb strips on to eight pre-soaked wooden
skewers. In a tray long enough to accommodate the skewers
lying down, mix together the marinade of yogurt, garlic, mint
and seasoning.

2 Put the meat in the marinade and turn until well coated.
Cover and leave to marinate for at least 1 hour but preferably
overnight in the refrigerator.

3 Preheat the grill to high and transfer the skewers to the grill
tray. Arrange the lemon wedges around the meat and brush
with the warm honey.

4 Grill for 4 minutes and then turn the brochettes and lemon.
Spoon any remaining marinade over the lamb and brush the
lemon with honey again. Grill for another 4 minutes or until the
lamb is just cooked through.

Tip... Always soak wooden skewers in water for
30 minutes before use to prevent them from burning.

Tangy chicken bruschetta

Serves 2
293 calories per serving
Takes 23 minutes

2 x 100 g (3½ oz) skinless
  boneless chicken breasts
2 tablespoons balsamic
  vinegar
½ teaspoon Dijon mustard
1 teaspoon clear honey
4 x 35 g slices rustic bread
75 g (2¾ oz) ready-made
  fresh, chunky tomato salsa
a small handful of watercress
salt and freshly ground black
  pepper

These zingy bruschetta make a perfect lunch or light meal.

1 Using a sharp knife, score the top of each chicken breast in about three places. In a non metallic bowl, mix together the vinegar, mustard, honey and seasoning. Add the chicken and turn to coat.

2 Preheat the grill to medium high and line the grill pan with foil. Remove the chicken from the marinade and grill for 15 minutes, turning halfway through the cooking time, until starting to caramelise and the juices run clear. Transfer to a board and slice thinly.

3 Grill the bread slices for 2 minutes, turning until toasted.

4 Top one side of each slice of toast with the tomato salsa and then top each with a quarter of the chicken and watercress. Serve immediately.

Variation... For a vegetarian version, use 3 x 52 g Quorn Fillets instead of the chicken and cook as above.

Prawn pâté with crispbreads

Serves 4
130 calories per serving
Takes 5 minutes

300 g (10½ oz) peeled cooked prawns, defrosted if frozen
100 g (3½ oz) cottage cheese
grated zest and juice of ½ a small lemon
a pinch of cayenne pepper
8 wholewheat crispbreads
75 g (2¾ oz) cucumber, sliced thinly
salt and freshly ground black pepper

Ideal for a super quick meal. And it's so good you'll still feel like you're spoiling yourself.

1 Reserve 50 g (1¾ oz) of the prawns to garnish and place the rest of the prawns in a food processor with the cottage cheese, lemon zest, lemon juice and cayenne pepper. Whizz to a thick paste. Season to taste.

2 Spread the pâté on to the crispbreads and top with the sliced cucumber and reserved prawns.

Pepperonata rigatoni

Serves 2
326 calories per serving
Takes 30 minutes

1 red pepper, halved and de-seeded

1 yellow or orange pepper, halved and de-seeded

125 g (4½ oz) dried rigatoni or penne

calorie controlled cooking spray

1 red onion, sliced thinly into rings

1 garlic clove, crushed

1 tablespoon thyme leaves

salt and freshly ground black pepper

15 g (½ oz) Parmesan cheese, grated, to serve

Pepperonata is a traditional antipasto dish, made of slowly cooked red and yellow or orange peppers. Stir this quick version into pasta and you have a delicious meal.

1 Preheat the grill to high. Lay the peppers skin side up on the grill pan and grill for 10 minutes until the skin is black and blistered. Place in a bowl, cover with cling film and leave to cool.

2 Bring a large pan of water to the boil, add the pasta and cook for 10–12 minutes or according to the packet instructions. Drain, reserving 2 tablespoons of the cooking liquid, and then rinse.

3 Spray a non stick frying pan with the cooking spray and heat. Add the onion and cook over a low heat for 10 minutes until softened and beginning to caramelise.

4 Meanwhile, peel the skin from the peppers, slice thinly and then add to the frying pan with the garlic and thyme. Season. Cook for a further 5 minutes. Add the reserved cooking liquid and then toss into the pasta and sprinkle with the Parmesan cheese.

Vegetable rosti cakes with rocket

Serves 4

165 calories per serving

Takes 10 minutes to prepare,
25 minutes to cook

350 g (12 oz) potatoes, peeled
1 teaspoon salt
225 g (8 oz) carrots, peeled
175 g (6 oz) fennel bulb,
shredded very finely
1 egg, beaten
1 tablespoon olive oil
1 tablespoon chopped fresh
parsley
calorie controlled cooking
spray
150 g (5½ oz) rocket
freshly ground black pepper

These make a tasty, filling light meal.

1 Coarsely grate the potatoes and place in a bowl. Sprinkle with the salt and leave to stand for 10 minutes (this helps draw out any excess moisture from the potatoes). Squeeze the potatoes, discarding the salty liquid, and place in a clean bowl.

2 Coarsely grate the carrots and add to the potato with the fennel, egg, oil and parsley. Season with black pepper and mix together thoroughly.

3 Spray a heavy based non stick frying pan with the cooking spray and heat. Cooking in two batches, drop 4 spoonfuls of the rosti mixture on to the pan and cook over a medium-low heat for 6–7 minutes per side. Repeat with the remaining mixture.

4 Pile equal amounts of rocket on to four serving plates and top each with two crispy cooked rosti. Serve at once.

Tip... For a more even-shaped rosti, place a metal cooking ring or pastry cutter in the frying pan. Press in a little of the rosti mixture and carefully remove the ring. Repeat with the remaining mixture.

Roast beef and horseradish cups

Serves 2
131 calories per serving
Takes 8 minutes

100 g (3½ oz) cooked roast
  beef, shredded
2 teaspoons Worcestershire
  sauce
½ small red onion, sliced
  finely
50 g (1¾ oz) roasted red
  peppers from a jar, drained
  and diced
50 g (1¾ oz) cherry tomatoes,
  halved
¼ cucumber, de-seeded
  and cut into very thin
  matchsticks
2 Little Gem lettuces, trimmed
  and outer leaves removed
1 tablespoon horseradish
  sauce
50 g (1¾ oz) 0% fat Greek
  yogurt
salt and freshly ground black
  pepper

Why not scatter over some home-made croûtons? Cut one
35 g slice of bread per person into cubes and pan-fry with
calorie controlled cooking spray until golden.

1 Put the beef in a bowl, add the Worcestershire sauce and
stir until coated. Stir in the onion, red peppers, cherry tomatoes
and cucumber. Remove eight large leaves from the lettuces
and arrange four on each plate.

2 Finely shred the remaining lettuce and mix it in with the beef
mixture. In a separate bowl, mix together the horseradish and
Greek yogurt. Season and then spoon a little into each lettuce
leaf, using it all up. Top each lettuce leaf with the beef mixture,
piling high, and serve immediately.

Ⓥ Variation... For a vegetarian version, replace the beef
with 7 x 14 g Quorn Peppered Beef Style Slices, shredded,
and omit the Worcestershire sauce.

Chinese prawn pancakes

Serves 4

165 calories per serving

Takes 30 minutes

250 g (9 oz) cooked peeled tiger prawns, defrosted if frozen
125 g (4½ oz) beansprouts
1 carrot, peeled and grated
75 g (2¾ oz) cucumber, diced finely
50 g (1¾ oz) radish, grated
½ x 25 g packet fresh coriander, chopped roughly
½ x 25 g packet fresh mint, chopped roughly
1 teaspoon caster sugar
1 tablespoon light soy sauce
juice of 2 limes
2 tablespoons sweet chilli sauce
1 teaspoon fish sauce
12 Chinese pancakes
lime wedges, to serve

A fresh, tasty light bite.

1 Put the prawns, beansprouts, carrot, cucumber, radish, coriander and mint in a large bowl.

2 In another small bowl, whisk together the sugar, soy sauce, lime juice, chilli sauce and fish sauce.

3 Pour the dressing over the prawn salad and toss to coat thoroughly.

4 Place a pancake on a board and put a generous spoonful of the prawn salad in the centre. Roll up and place seam side down on a serving plate. Repeat with the remaining pancakes and prawn salad. Serve three pancakes each immediately, with lime wedges on the side.

Spicy turkey cakes with fresh tomato salsa

Serves 4
150 calories per serving
Takes 40 minutes

350 g (12 oz) minced turkey
2 teaspoons Thai red curry paste
1 egg, beaten
2 tablespoons cornflour
grated zest of 2 limes
a small bunch of fresh coriander, chopped
2 spring onions, sliced finely
1 red chilli, de-seeded and sliced finely
calorie controlled cooking spray
lime wedges, to serve

For the salsa

2 ripe tomatoes, quartered, de-seeded and diced finely
½ red pepper, de-seeded and diced
juice of 2 limes
1 small red onion, diced finely
1 small red chilli, de-seeded and diced finely

These little cakes are good for a light lunch or appetiser with drinks. Serve with a fresh tomato, red onion and red pepper salsa with lots of lime juice and lime wedges.

1 Put the minced turkey, red curry paste and about half the egg in a food processor and whizz until evenly blended. Transfer to a bowl.

2 Add the cornflour, lime zest, coriander, spring onions and chilli and mix well with your fingers. Add more egg if necessary to bind the mixture.

3 Using wet hands, divide the mixture into 12 portions. Roll each into a ball and then flatten slightly to make a patty.

4 Heat a large non stick frying pan and spray with the cooking spray. Fry the cakes in batches for about 5 minutes on each side, until golden and cooked through.

5 Meanwhile, place all the salsa ingredients in a bowl and toss together to mix thoroughly. Serve with the turkey cakes and lime wedges.

Variation... Try serving these turkey cakes with a soy dipping sauce and/or some sweet chilli sauce.

Smoked salmon pinwheels with roasted asparagus

Serves 4
118 calories per serving
Takes 10 minutes

200 g (7 oz) fine asparagus tips
2 tablespoons balsamic vinegar
200 g (7 oz) thinly sliced smoked salmon
100 g (3½ oz) low fat soft cheese
salt and freshly ground black pepper
1 lemon, cut into wedges, to serve

English asparagus has a relatively short season – May to June – but it's worth looking out for. Not only does it taste better and cost less than the imported varieties, but it'll be fresher. Roasting asparagus, as opposed to steaming or boiling it, helps to bring out the flavour.

1 Preheat the oven to Gas Mark 6/200°C/fan oven 180°C. Place the asparagus tips in a shallow non stick roasting tray.

2 Drizzle over the balsamic vinegar, season and roast in the oven for 5 minutes until just tender.

3 Lay a strip of the smoked salmon on a work surface and spread with a little soft cheese. Place three to four asparagus tips at one end of the strip and roll them up until they are enclosed in the salmon.

4 Place on a serving plate and repeat with the other salmon slices and asparagus. Serve scattered with black pepper and with lemon wedges to squeeze over.

Perfect poultry

Chicken with olives and oregano

Serves 4

220 calories per serving

Takes 10 minutes to prepare,
1 hour 10 minutes to cook

❄

calorie controlled cooking
spray

**400 g (14 oz) skinless chicken
drumsticks**

**400 g (14 oz) skinless chicken
thighs**

**1 red pepper, de-seeded and
cut into strips**

**1 yellow pepper, de-seeded
and cut into strips**

4 plum tomatoes, halved

**50 g (1¾ oz) stoned black
olives in brine, drained**

2 garlic cloves, sliced

**1 bay leaf and 2 fresh oregano
sprigs, tied together**

**450 ml (16 fl oz) hot chicken
stock**

**salt and freshly ground black
pepper**

**2 tablespoons chopped fresh
parsley, to garnish**

*This Italian-style chicken casserole is a great make
ahead supper. Serve with 125 g (4½ oz) potatoes, mashed
with 1 tablespoon of skimmed milk, per person.*

1 Preheat the oven to Gas Mark 4/180°C/fan oven 160°C.
Spray a large, lidded, ovenproof casserole dish with the
cooking spray and heat until hot. Add the chicken drumsticks
and thighs and cook until brown. You may need to do this in
batches. Remove with a slotted spoon and keep warm. Add the
peppers to the dish and cook for 2–3 minutes until softened.

2 Add all the remaining ingredients except the garnish, but
including the chicken, to the pan. Bring to the boil, cover and
cook in the oven for an hour until the chicken is falling from the
bone. Season.

3 Serve garnished with the parsley.

Variation... If you prefer, you could use a 400 g can of whole
tomatoes, instead of the fresh ones.

Honeyed duck bowl

Serves 2
390 calories per serving
Takes 20 minutes

calorie controlled cooking
spray
150 g (5½ oz) skinless
boneless duck breast
2 rounded teaspoons clear
honey
150 g (5½ oz) baby corn,
sliced diagonally
125 g (4½ oz) dried medium
egg noodles
2.5 cm (1 inch) fresh root
ginger, cut into matchsticks
1 tablespoon soy sauce
850 ml (1½ pints) hot chicken
stock
50 g (1¾ oz) baby spinach,
washed
2 spring onions, sliced
diagonally

This delicious Oriental-style dish is a complete meal-in-a-bowl.

1 Heat a non stick frying pan until hot and spray with the cooking spray. Pan-fry the duck breast for 6 minutes on each side over a medium heat. Add the honey, immediately remove the pan from the hob and turn the duck over several times to coat in the honey. Set aside for 5 minutes.

2 Meanwhile, bring a pan of water to the boil, add the baby corn and noodles and cook for 4 minutes or until tender. While they are cooking, add the ginger and soy sauce to the chicken stock and set aside for the ginger to infuse.

3 Drain the noodles and corn and divide between two deep bowls. Top with the spinach and spring onions and pour the gingered stock all over.

4 Slice the duck breast thinly and arrange on top of the noodles and vegetables, drizzling with any juices from the pan.

Variation... Try lean pork fillet instead of duck. Slice 150 g (5½ oz) of pork fillet thinly and dust with 1 teaspoon of Chinese five spice. Fry for 3–4 minutes on each side in step 1 until cooked through but still juicy.

Chicken and spring vegetable fricassee

Serves 4
335 calories per serving
Takes 30 minutes

4 x 150 g (5½ oz) skinless boneless chicken breasts
250 g (9 oz) low fat soft cheese with garlic and herbs
calorie controlled cooking spray
2 garlic cloves, crushed
200 g (7 oz) baby carrots, scrubbed and trimmed
200 g (7 oz) button onions
200 g (7 oz) baby turnips, peeled and halved, or baby corn, halved
425 ml (15 fl oz) vegetable stock
½ cauliflower, sliced into small florets
½ head of broccoli, sliced into small florets
a small bunch of fresh tarragon or parsley, chopped (optional)
4 tablespoons virtually fat free plain fromage frais
salt and freshly ground black pepper

Make the most of baby vegetables with this dish.

1 With a sharp knife, make a deep incision into the side of each chicken breast. Push a teaspoon of the soft cheese into each slit. Heat a large, lidded, flameproof casserole dish or pan, spray with the cooking spray and season. Brown the chicken breasts on both sides and then remove to a plate.

2 Spray the pan again and add the garlic, carrots, onions and turnips or baby corn. Brown them all over for 5 minutes.

3 Return the chicken to the casserole and add the stock. Bring to the boil, scraping up any stuck on juices from the bottom of the pan with a wooden spatula. Cover and simmer for 10 minutes.

4 Add the cauliflower, broccoli, tarragon or parsley, if using, and the remaining soft cheese. Season, cover and simmer for a further 5–10 minutes, until the cauliflower is tender and the chicken is cooked through.

5 Allow to cool a little and then stir in the fromage frais and serve.

Pot roast turkey with autumn vegetables

Serves 4

365 calories per serving

Takes 20 minutes to prepare,
   1 hour to cook

calorie controlled cooking
   spray

1 kg (2 lb 4 oz) turkey breast
   joint

1 whole garlic bulb, halved
   horizontally

1 lemon, halved

300 ml (10 fl oz) chicken or
   vegetable stock

a small bunch of fresh thyme,
   tough stems removed and
   leaves chopped

2 carrots, peeled and thickly
   sliced diagonally

1 pumpkin or butternut
   squash, peeled, de-seeded
   and cut into large chunks

1 celeriac, peeled and cut into
   chunks

1 large courgette, cut into
   chunks

salt and freshly ground black
   pepper

*Pot-roasting a turkey breast joint like this guarantees
moist and tender meat, and it's wonderfully simple.*

1 Preheat the oven to Gas Mark 4/180°C/fan oven 160°C. Heat
a large, lidded, flameproof casserole dish and spray with the
cooking spray. Add the joint and brown it all over. Remove to a
plate.

2 Add the garlic, lemon and stock, half of the thyme and some
of the vegetables, except the courgette, enough to cover the
bottom of the casserole dish. Place the turkey back on top.
Season, cover and roast in the oven for 45 minutes.

3 Meanwhile, place the rest of the carrots, pumpkin or
butternut squash and celeriac in a non stick roasting tray with
the remaining thyme, spray with the cooking spray and season.
Roast for 45 minutes below the casserole. After 25 minutes add
the courgette to the roasting tray, spraying it with the cooking
spray. When the vegetables are cooked, keep them warm.

4 Lift the turkey out of the casserole dish on to a carving
board. Cover with foil and allow it to rest. Spoon all the
vegetables into a serving dish and drain the juices into a
serving jug, draining off the fat. Check the seasoning and serve
three skinless slices of turkey per person with the vegetables
and juices.

Hearty turkey casserole

Serves 4

293 calories per serving

Takes 15 minutes to prepare,
30 minutes to cook

✳

calorie controlled cooking
spray

**500 g (1 lb 2 oz) skinless
boneless turkey breast,
diced**

2 large leeks, sliced thickly

**400 g (14 oz) butternut
squash, peeled, de-seeded
and chopped roughly**

**2 tablespoons plain white
flour**

**425 ml (15 fl oz) hot chicken
stock**

**40 g (1½ oz) dried Puy lentils,
rinsed**

**1 teaspoon dried tarragon or
1 tablespoon chopped fresh
tarragon**

**2 tablespoons half fat crème
fraîche**

freshly ground black pepper

*Serve with 200 g (7 oz) potatoes, mashed with
2 tablespoons of skimmed milk, per person.*

1 Heat a large, lidded, flameproof casserole dish on the hob
and spray with the cooking spray. Season the turkey with black
pepper, add to the casserole and brown for 4 minutes, stirring
occasionally. This may need to be done in batches.

2 Add the leeks to the casserole, cook for 2 minutes and
then stir in the butternut squash and flour, mixing well to
coat. Gradually blend in the stock and mix in the Puy lentils
and tarragon. Bring to a simmer, cover and cook gently for
30 minutes until tender.

3 Stir in the crème fraîche just before serving.

Variation... Why not try using the same weight of diced,
skinless, boneless chicken breast?

Tequila chicken

Serves 6

203 calories per serving

Takes 20 minutes to prepare + marinating, 20 minutes to cook

3 tablespoons tequila

4 rounded teaspoons clear honey

finely grated zest and juice of a lime

6 x 125 g (4½ oz) skinless boneless chicken breasts

freshly ground black pepper

For the salsa

2 x 125 g (4½ oz) corn on the cob

calorie controlled cooking spray

1 red pepper, de-seeded and diced

3 heaped tablespoons chopped fresh coriander

1 small red onion, chopped finely

1 lime

A vibrantly coloured dish that looks wonderful on the plate.

1 Stir the tequila, honey, lime zest and lime juice together in a small bowl. Season with black pepper and pour into a large plastic food bag. Slash each chicken breast a few times and add to the marinade, turning to coat. Seal the bag and marinate in the fridge for at least 30 minutes. Preheat the oven to Gas Mark 6/200°C/fan oven 180°C.

2 Meanwhile, for the salsa, preheat the grill to medium high and spray the corn on the cob with the cooking spray. Grill for 15 minutes, turning to colour evenly. Leave to cool and then slice the toasted corn kernels away from the cob. Mix the corn with the pepper, coriander and red onion. Finely grate the zest from half the lime and add to the salsa, along with the squeezed juice of the whole lime.

3 Remove the chicken from its marinade and place on a non stick baking tray. Cook in the oven for 20 minutes or until cooked, glazing with some of the marinade halfway through. Serve with the salsa spooned over the chicken.

Variation... If you don't have any tequila, you can use vodka or whisky in the marinade instead.

Chicken kebabs with fresh carrot relish

Serves 4

160 calories per serving

Takes 10 minutes to prepare,
15 minutes to cook

1 red onion, quartered

4 x 125 g (4½ oz) skinless boneless chicken breasts, cut into 2 cm (¾ inch) cubes

½ teaspoon dried mixed herbs

1 green pepper, de-seeded and cut into 2 cm (¾ inch) cubes

salt and freshly ground black pepper

For the carrot relish

2 carrots, peeled and grated coarsely

juice of a small lemon

1 tablespoon chopped fresh mint or parsley

These tangy and refreshing kebabs are great cooked on the barbecue in summer.

1 First make the relish. Mix the carrots with the lemon juice, mint or parsley and seasoning. Let it stand for 10–15 minutes to allow the carrots to soften.

2 Meanwhile, divide the onion into its individual layers. Sprinkle the chicken with the dried herbs and mix well to coat the pieces. Thread the meat, onion and pepper, in turn, on to four skewers and season lightly. Preheat the grill.

3 Grill the kebabs for about 12 minutes, turning them once. Keep a mug of water at the ready and brush the meat as it cooks – do this about three or four times during cooking as it helps to moisten the meat. When cooked, the meat should feel firm when pressed.

4 Divide the relish between four plates. Serve the kebabs on top.

Variations... Fresh vegetable relishes make excellent accompaniments. Try finely chopped cucumber and tomato; add some seasoning, a pinch or two of ground cumin and some chopped fresh parsley or mint. Allow to stand for 10 minutes before serving.

Ⓥ For a vegetarian alternative, substitute Quorn Chicken Style Pieces for the chicken.

Duck in cherry sauce with polenta

Serves 2

319 calories per serving

Takes 45 minutes + cooling

**calorie controlled cooking
spray**

200 ml (7 fl oz) chicken stock

2 drops Tabasco sauce

**50 g (1¾ oz) dried quick-cook
polenta**

**20 g (¾ oz) spinach, washed
and chopped**

**200 g (7 oz) fresh cherries,
stoned and halved**

½ tablespoon lemon juice

**½ tablespoon artificial
sweetener**

**2 x 150 g (5½ oz) skinless
boneless duck breasts**

salt

Serve this fantastic dish with steamed green beans.

1 Spray a small tin or dish with the cooking spray. Bring the chicken stock to the boil in a saucepan with the Tabasco sauce and season with salt. Add the polenta, reduce the heat to very low and cook for 4 minutes. It will look like very thick mashed potato. Stir in the spinach, cook for a further minute and then spoon the mixture into the prepared tin or dish. Allow to cool for at least half an hour (or overnight).

2 Put the cherries in a small pan with the lemon juice, sweetener, a pinch of salt and a tablespoon of water. Gently cook for 5 minutes and then set aside.

3 Heat a non stick frying pan on a high heat and spray with the cooking spray. Add the duck breasts and reduce the heat to medium. Fry the duck breasts for 3–4 minutes on each side for pink meat and up to 7 minutes on each side if you prefer the meat well done. Meanwhile, reheat the cherry sauce.

4 When cooked, remove the duck and leave it to rest. Turn the pan heat up, spray with the cooking spray, slice the polenta into two pieces and fry them in the pan until golden on both sides.

5 To serve, put the duck and polenta on two plates and pour the cherry sauce over.

Tip... You can buy a cherry pitter from cookshops and some supermarkets. It makes taking the stones out of cherries and olives quicker, easier and a lot less messy.

Chicken with black bean and pineapple salsa

Serves 4
205 calories per serving
Takes 25 minutes

450 g (1 lb) skinless boneless chicken breasts
1 garlic clove, halved
calorie controlled cooking spray
salt and freshly ground black pepper

For the salsa

1 red onion, chopped very finely
2 tablespoons red wine vinegar
1 teaspoon caster sugar
2 teaspoons extra virgin olive oil
3 tablespoons chopped fresh parsley
100 g (3½ oz) drained canned pineapple in natural juice, chopped finely
125 g (4½ oz) drained canned black beans, rinsed

Salsas are an excellent way to liven up grilled meat, chicken or fish, and this one is particularly good.

1 Preheat the grill to medium. Season the chicken breasts and rub the cut sides of the halved garlic over each breast. Spray with the cooking spray. Place the chicken under the grill and cook for 5–6 minutes on each side, until it is cooked through.

2 Meanwhile, make the salsa. Place the red onion in a mixing bowl with the vinegar, sugar, olive oil and parsley and stir well. Add the pineapple and black beans and mix together thoroughly. Cover the bowl and leave it to stand until you are ready to serve it with the grilled chicken.

Variation... There are a huge variety of canned beans available in shops these days; the black beans in this recipe contrast wonderfully against the red onion and green parsley. Try experimenting with other varieties such as kidney or borlotti beans.

Baked Mediterranean turkey

Serves 2

520 calories per serving

Takes 20 minutes to prepare,
20 minutes to cook

2 x 125 g (4½ oz) skinless
boneless turkey breast
steaks

grated zest and juice of a
lemon

2 teaspoons dried oregano

2 teaspoons olive oil

salt and freshly ground black
pepper

a small bunch of fresh
parsley, chopped, to garnish
(optional)

For the couscous

175 g (6 oz) dried couscous

600 ml (20 fl oz) boiling stock

100 g (3½ oz) cooked beetroot,
diced

1 small red onion, diced

*A very quick, fresh-tasting dish, best served with a
summery salad.*

1 Preheat the oven to Gas Mark 6/200°C/fan oven 180°C and
place the turkey steaks on two separate pieces of foil large
enough to completely wrap them up.

2 Season, sprinkle half the lemon zest, lemon juice and herbs
on each turkey steak and drizzle each with a teaspoon of oil.
Seal in the foil, place on a baking tray and bake for 20 minutes.

3 Meanwhile, place the couscous in a bowl and pour over the
boiling stock. Cover with cling film and leave to steam for at
least 10 minutes.

4 Fluff up the couscous with a fork and stir in the diced
beetroot and red onion.

5 Unwrap the turkey and put on plates with the juices left in
the foil poured over. Serve with the couscous and sprinkled
with the parsley, if using.

Variation... You could serve a herby pasta with the turkey if
you prefer, instead of the beetroot couscous.

Braised Italian chicken

Serves 4

330 calories per serving

Takes 35 minutes to prepare,
1½ hours to cook

1.5 kg (3 lb 5 oz) whole chicken

calorie controlled cooking spray

3 garlic cloves, halved horizontally

1 onion, chopped roughly

2 small fennel bulbs, cut into chunks

2 parsnips (total 180 g/6 oz), peeled and cut into chunks

5 preserved lemons from a jar, drained and halved

4 fresh thyme sprigs, plus extra to garnish

450 ml (16 fl oz) chicken stock

125 ml (4 fl oz) limoncello

freshly ground black pepper

Limoncello is an Italian lemon liqueur and when simmered slowly it gives the chicken a zesty sweet sauce.

1 Heat a large, lidded, flameproof casserole dish until hot and spray the chicken with the cooking spray. Brown the chicken for 5–8 minutes, turning until brown on all sides. Remove and set aside. Spray the pan again with the cooking spray and add the garlic, onion, fennel and parsnips. Cook gently for 8–10 minutes until starting to soften and browned.

2 Put half the preserved lemons and the thyme sprigs into the chicken cavity. Return the chicken to the casserole dish and scatter over the remaining lemons. Pour over the chicken stock and limoncello. Bring to the boil. Cover with foil, add the lid and gently simmer for 1½ hours until the chicken is cooked.

3 To serve, remove the chicken from the dish and cover loosely with foil to rest. Using a slotted spoon, remove the vegetables and keep warm. Bring the cooking liquid to the boil and bubble rapidly for 5–10 minutes until reduced by half and thickened. Check the seasoning and pour into a jug. Allow it to settle and then spoon off any fat. Remove the chicken skin and discard, carve the chicken into slices and serve 120 g (4½ oz) per person with the vegetables and sauce. Garnish with the extra thyme and black pepper.

Chicken and duck terrine

Serves 8
287 calories per serving
Takes 30 minutes to prepare + overnight chilling, 1½ hours to cook ❄

Although this is a terrine, it makes a great dinner party main course when served with a salad and 110 g (4 oz) cooked new potatoes per person. It's not difficult and the end result is impressive.

2 x 150 g (5½ oz) skinless boneless chicken breasts
2 x 150 g (5½ oz) skinless boneless duck breasts
100 ml (3½ fl oz) port
250 g (9 oz) lean minced pork
2 tablespoons chopped fresh tarragon
grated zest of a small orange
1 egg

1 egg white
25 g (1 oz) stoned green or black olives in brine, drained and chopped
12 rashers smoked streaky bacon
125 g (4½ oz) sweet peppers from a jar, drained and cut into strips
calorie controlled cooking spray
salt and freshly ground black pepper

1 Cut the chicken breasts and one of the duck breasts into four equal strips. Place in a non metallic dish and marinate in the port for 10 minutes.

2 Cut the remaining duck breast into small pieces. Place in a bowl with the minced pork, tarragon, orange zest, egg, egg white and olives. Mix well and season.

3 Preheat the oven to Gas Mark 2/150°C/fan oven 130°C. Line a 900 g (2 lb) loaf tin with the bacon rashers, ensuring they meet and overlap on the base and overhang the edges enough to cover the contents. You don't need to cover the ends of the tin.

continues overleaf ▶

4 Drain the chicken and duck breasts, pouring any excess marinade into the pork mixture and mixing well. Spoon half the pork mixture into the tin. Lay the chicken and duck pieces on top, pressing down to level the surface. Arrange the strips of pepper evenly over the surface and spread with the remaining pork mixture.

5 Fold the overhanging bacon rashers over the top. Spray some foil with the cooking spray and use to cover the loaf tin, sprayed side down. Place on a baking tray and bake for 1½ hours.

6 Remove from the oven and pour off about half the liquid in the loaf tin. Cool and then chill overnight with weights (use cans) on top to press it down. Serve cold or reheat in a microwave until piping hot.

Tips... Store in the fridge, wrapped in cling film, for up to 5 days or wrap and freeze.

Individual portions can be used for a lunchbox.

Variations... Duck breasts are expensive so you could replace them with chicken breasts, although the flavour will not be quite so gamey.

Thyme works just as well as tarragon in this recipe.

Sesame and pepper chicken parcels

Serves 4

170 calories per serving

Takes 25 minutes to prepare +
20 minutes marinating,
20 minutes to cook

❄

2 tablespoons dark soy sauce

1 teaspoon sesame oil

1 garlic clove, crushed

1 teaspoon tomato purée

350 g (12 oz) skinless
boneless chicken breasts,
cut into long thin strips

1 tablespoon sesame seeds

8 spring onions

1 red pepper, de-seeded and
sliced thinly

1 green pepper, de-seeded and
sliced thinly

150 g (5½ oz) carrots, peeled
and cut into matchsticks

*This is a really colourful and attractive way of serving
chicken, adding a bit of fun to the occasion.*

1 In a bowl, mix together the soy sauce, sesame oil, crushed
garlic and tomato purée. Add the chicken and mix well. Cover
and leave to marinate for 20 minutes.

2 Place the sesame seeds in a small saucepan and heat until
they turn golden brown. Remove and set them aside.

3 Trim the spring onions, so that you are just left with the
green part, and then slice thinly. Add the peppers, carrots and
the spring onions to the chicken mixture, stirring well.

4 Divide the chicken and vegetables into four portions. Cut
four squares of greaseproof paper big enough to parcel up
each portion. Spoon the chicken mixture on to the squares and
wrap each parcel up tightly. Arrange the parcels in a steamer
and cook for 20 minutes.

5 Carefully lift the parcels out of the steamer and unwrap
them. Scatter over the toasted sesame seeds and transfer the
parcels to four warmed plates to serve.

Tip... If you don't have a steamer, put the parcels in a metal
colander or sieve and place over a saucepan of simmering
water. Cover the top tightly to prevent the steam from
escaping.

Turkey steaks with orange and watercress

Serves 4

275 calories per serving

Takes 10 minutes to prepare,
 15 minutes to cook

**4 x 150 g (5½ oz) skinless
 boneless turkey steaks**

1 tablespoon olive oil

**finely grated zest and juice of
 an orange**

2 tablespoons clear honey

2 teaspoons cumin seeds

**175 g (6 oz) sugar snap peas
 or mange tout**

**175 g (6 oz) carrots, peeled
 and cut into very thin slices**

**175 g (6 oz) asparagus or fine
 green beans**

**salt and freshly ground black
 pepper**

To garnish

a few watercress sprigs

shreds of orange zest

Zingy turkey and vegetables will brighten up any day.

1 Preheat the grill to high. Arrange the turkey steaks on the grill rack and season.

2 Mix together the oil, orange zest, orange juice, honey and cumin seeds. Use half this mixture to brush over the turkey steaks. Grill them on each side for 6–8 minutes until thoroughly cooked, basting often.

3 Meanwhile, bring a pan of water to the boil, add the vegetables and cook until just tender. Drain well and add the reserved orange mixture. Reheat for a few moments.

4 Divide the vegetables between four warmed serving plates and serve with the turkey steaks. Garnish with watercress and shreds of orange zest.

Tip... If you wish, marinate the turkey steaks in the orange juice mixture to impart a more pronounced flavour.

Variation... You could use skinless boneless chicken breasts instead of the turkey steaks.

Marvellous meat

Beef Wellington

Serves 4
341 calories per serving
Takes 40 minutes
❄

Tender beef fillet wrapped in filo pastry with a quick mushroom pâté makes an impressive dinner party main course. Serve with steamed green beans.

400 g (14 oz) beef fillet, trimmed of visible fat

calorie controlled cooking spray

200 g (7 oz) mushrooms, chopped finely

2 shallots, chopped finely

150 g (5½ oz) low fat soft cheese

1 tablespoon chopped fresh tarragon

12 x 15 g (½ oz) sheets filo pastry, measuring 30 x 40 cm (12 x 16 inches)

salt and freshly ground black pepper

1 Preheat the oven to Gas Mark 7/220°C/fan oven 200°C.

2 Cut the beef into four equal portions and season. Lightly spray a non stick frying pan with the cooking spray and heat until hot. Add the beef and cook for 3–4 minutes until browned all over. Remove from the pan and set aside.

3 Spray the pan again with the cooking spray and add the mushrooms and shallots. Cook, stirring, for 10 minutes over a medium heat until the mushroom juices have been released and evaporated.

4 Place the soft cheese in a bowl and beat until smooth. Add the mushroom mixture and tarragon and mix well. Lightly spray a baking tray with the cooking spray.

5 Lay one sheet of filo pastry on a board and spray with the cooking spray. Add another sheet and spray that, topping with a final sheet. Place a piece of beef in the middle of the sheets, spoon on a quarter of the mushroom mixture and wrap up. You can either do this neatly, as you would wrap a parcel, or bring up the sides and scrunch the top, making sure you seal in the contents. Carefully place on the baking tray and spray with the cooking spray. Repeat to make four parcels.

6 Bake the parcels for 10 minutes until the pastry is golden and crispy.

Citrus pork steaks with potato salad

Serves 4
385 calories per serving
Takes 25 minutes

700 g (1 lb 9 oz) small new potatoes, scrubbed and halved

250 g (9 oz) fine green beans, halved

1½ teaspoons peppercorns, crushed

finely grated zest and juice of an orange

4 x 125 g (4½ oz) lean pork loin steaks, trimmed of visible fat

calorie controlled cooking spray

juice of ½ a lemon

2 rounded teaspoons clear honey

3 tablespoons low fat French dressing

A smart dish for a kitchen supper with friends.

1 Bring a large pan of water to the boil, add the potatoes and cook for 12–15 minutes or until almost tender. Add the green beans and cook for a further 5 minutes. Drain thoroughly.

2 Meanwhile, mix the crushed peppercorns with the orange zest and press on to the pork steaks. Heat a non stick frying pan until hot and spray with the cooking spray. Fry the pork steaks for 5 minutes on each side and then add the orange juice, lemon juice, honey and 2 tablespoons of water. Bubble gently for 2 minutes.

3 Toss the potatoes and beans with the French dressing. Serve the pork steaks with the warm potato and bean salad and the pan juices drizzled on top.

Minty lamb nuggets with pea mayo

Serves 4

350 calories per serving

Takes 30 minutes

❄ (nuggets only, at the end
of step 2, before cooking)

400 g (14 oz) potatoes, peeled
and cut into ½ cm (¼ inch)
chips

calorie controlled cooking
spray

3 spring onions, chopped
finely

2 teaspoons dried mint

500 g (1 lb 2 oz) lean minced
lamb

50 g (1¾ oz) dried natural
breadcrumbs

100 g (3½ oz) frozen peas,
defrosted

50 g (1¾ oz) low fat soft
cheese

1 tablespoon reduced fat
mayonnaise

salt and freshly ground black
pepper

Serve with a generous tomato side salad.

1 Preheat the oven to Gas Mark 7/220°C/fan oven 200°C. Put the potatoes on a large non stick baking tray and spray with the cooking spray. Bake in the oven for 10 minutes.

2 Meanwhile, mix together the spring onions, 1 teaspoon of the mint, the lamb and 15 g (½ oz) of the breadcrumbs in a bowl. Season. With wet hands, shape into 24 nuggets of the same size. Put the remaining breadcrumbs on a plate and roll the nuggets in the breadcrumbs to coat.

3 Remove the potatoes from the oven and turn them over, moving them slightly over to one side on the tray. Add the lamb nuggets, return to the oven and cook for 10–15 minutes until the nuggets are cooked through and the potatoes are golden.

4 Meanwhile, to make the pea mayo, put the peas, soft cheese, mayonnaise, remaining mint and seasoning in a food processor. Whizz until nearly smooth. Serve the lamb nuggets with the potatoes and pea mayo.

Mango masala lamb steaks

Serves 4
385 calories per serving
Takes 30 minutes

900 g (2 lb) potatoes, peeled
   and cut into 1 cm (½ inch)
   dice
calorie controlled cooking
   spray
1 onion, sliced
1 green chilli, de-seeded and
   sliced
2 teaspoons cumin seeds
2 teaspoons garam masala
4 x 125 g (4½ oz) lean lamb
   leg steaks, trimmed of
   visible fat
80 g (3 oz) mango chutney

*A quick spice rub and a chutney topping give these lamb
steaks a fantastic flavour.*

1 Bring a pan of water to the boil, add the potatoes and parboil
for 7 minutes. Drain and shake the potatoes to roughen the
edges slightly.

2 While the potatoes are cooking, heat a large non stick
frying pan, spray with the cooking spray and cook the onion
for 5 minutes, adding 1 tablespoon of water to help soften the
onion.

3 Stir the potatoes, chilli and half of the cumin seeds in with
the onion. Cook, stirring occasionally, for 15 minutes until
tender and crisp.

4 Meanwhile, preheat the grill to medium high. Mix the rest
of the cumin seeds with the garam masala. Spray the lamb
with the cooking spray and coat in the spice mixture. Grill for
6 minutes and then turn and grill for another 2 minutes. Top
each lamb steak with chutney and cook for a final 4 minutes.

5 Serve the lamb with the crisp, spiced potatoes.

Tip... Shaking parboiled potatoes in the pan roughens up
the edges and creates more surface area for crisping up
when pan-fried.

Italian pork-stuffed courgettes

Serves 4

295 calories per serving

Takes 30 minutes to prepare,
20 minutes to cook

❄

8 courgettes

calorie controlled cooking
spray

1 small onion, chopped finely

2 garlic cloves, chopped finely

400 g (14 oz) lean minced pork

4 fresh rosemary sprigs,
leaves chopped finely

grated zest and juice of a
lemon

2 tablespoons Worcestershire
sauce

2 medium slices white bread

a bunch of fresh parsley,
chopped

salt and freshly ground black
pepper

A wonderfully evocative recipe that is simple to make.
Serve with a mixed salad.

1 Preheat the oven to Gas Mark 4/180°C/fan oven 160°C.
Cut the courgettes in half lengthways and scrape out the seeds
with a teaspoon but reserve. Heat a non stick frying pan and
spray with the cooking spray. Fry the onion and garlic for
4 minutes until softened.

2 Add the minced pork and season well. Stir until browned all
over and then add the courgette seeds, rosemary, lemon zest,
lemon juice and Worcestershire sauce. Cook for 2–3 minutes.
Using a food processor, whizz the bread to breadcrumbs.

3 Spray a non stick baking tray with the cooking spray and put
the courgettes on it with their hollowed out sides up. Spoon in
the mince mixture and press down with the back of the spoon.
Mix together the breadcrumbs and parsley, season and sprinkle
over the top of the mince.

4 Bake for 20 minutes or until golden brown and crispy.

Chorizo lasagne

Serves 4

352 calories per serving

Takes 40 minutes to prepare,
30–35 minutes to cook

❄

400 g (14 oz) butternut
squash, peeled, de-seeded
and cut into medium size
chunks

1 red onion, cut into wedges

1 red pepper, de-seeded and
cut into chunks

1 courgette, cut into chunks

calorie controlled cooking
spray

50 g (1¾ oz) chorizo sausage,
chopped

12 cherry tomatoes, halved

500 g jar tomato sauce for
pasta

6 dried no-precook lasagne
sheets (about 120 g/4½ oz
in total)

40 g packet Cheddar cheese
sauce mix

300 ml (10 fl oz) skimmed milk

salt and freshly ground black
pepper

*This is a wonderful twist on a traditional recipe. It's full of
flavour and sure to be a big hit.*

1 Preheat the oven to Gas Mark 6/200°C/fan oven 180°C.

2 Put the squash, onion, pepper and courgette in a large non
stick roasting tin and spray with the cooking spray. Season and
toss to coat. Roast for 15 minutes and then add the chorizo.
Stir well and roast for 5–10 minutes more, until the vegetables
are tender.

3 Add the tomatoes to the vegetables and then stir in the
tomato sauce.

4 Tip half of the vegetable mixture into a large rectangular
baking dish, measuring about 25 x 20 cm (10 x 8 inches).
Arrange three lasagne sheets on top. Repeat the layers.

5 Make the cheese sauce with the skimmed milk, following
the packet instructions. Pour evenly over the top of the lasagne.
Bake for 30–35 minutes, until golden brown. Remove from the
oven and allow to stand for a few minutes before serving.

Gingered beef with sweet potato mash

Serves 4
366 calories per serving
Takes 25 minutes

750 g (1 lb 10 oz) sweet
    potatoes, peeled and diced
    roughly
1 tablespoon grated fresh root
    ginger
2 heaped teaspoons clear
    honey
finely grated zest and juice of
    ½ a lime
4 x 110 g (4 oz) lean beef
    medallion steaks, trimmed of
    visible fat
calorie controlled cooking
    spray
2 teaspoons low fat spread
salt and freshly ground black
    pepper

*Sweet potato mash makes a nice change and has a
luxurious velvety texture. Serve with sugar snap peas.*

1 Bring a pan of water to the boil, add the sweet potatoes and
cook for 12–15 minutes until tender.

2 Meanwhile, make a paste from half the ginger, the honey,
lime zest and lime juice. Spread over the steaks on both sides
and set aside for 5–10 minutes.

3 Spray a non stick frying pan with the cooking spray and
pan-fry the steaks for 2–3 minutes on each side, or until
cooked to your liking.

4 Drain the sweet potatoes in a colander. Melt the low fat
spread in the saucepan, add the remaining ginger and cook for
30 seconds until aromatic. Return the potatoes to the pan and
mash with the ginger. Season to taste and serve with the beef
steaks.

Summery pork mince

Serves 4

455 calories per serving

Takes 15 minutes to prepare, 35 minutes to cook

❄ (at the end of step 2, after cooling)

Lean mince is very practical for family meals, but it's easy to get stuck in a rut, cooking the same few dishes. This citrusy mince sauce has a delightfully fresh flavour and can also be served with spaghetti (250 g/9 oz dried weight for four people, cooked according to the packet instructions) instead of with rice.

calorie controlled cooking spray

500 g (1 lb 2 oz) lean minced pork

2 carrots, peeled and grated coarsely

1 courgette, grated coarsely

2 garlic cloves, crushed

2 tablespoons chopped fresh lemon thyme

finely grated zest and juice of a lemon

15 g (½ oz) plain white flour

400 ml (14 fl oz) hot chicken stock

250 g (9 oz) dried brown basmati rice

600 ml (20 fl oz) boiling water

150 g (5½ oz) fine green beans

1 Heat a lidded flameproof casserole dish on the hob and spray with the cooking spray. Add the minced pork and brown for 5 minutes, stirring to break it up. Add the carrots, courgette, garlic and thyme, plus the lemon zest. Cook for 2 minutes, stirring.

2 Add the flour, half the lemon juice and the stock. Bring to a simmer, cover and cook for 20 minutes.

3 Meanwhile, place the rice, boiling water and the rest of the lemon juice in a large lidded saucepan and bring to the boil. Stir once and then cover and reduce the heat to the lowest setting. Cook undisturbed for 25 minutes until the rice is tender and the liquid has been absorbed.

4 Add the green beans to the casserole and replace the lid. Cook for 10 minutes until tender. Serve ladled over the lemon rice.

Tip... Make large batches of recipes like this and then freeze portions ready for an easy meal when you don't have the time or inclination to cook.

Creamy steak dauphinois

Serves 2

345 calories per serving

Takes 30 minutes to prepare + cooling, 20 minutes to cook

2 x 150 g (5½ oz) lean fillet steaks, trimmed of visible fat and slightly flattened

calorie controlled cooking spray

175 g (6 oz) potato, peeled and sliced thinly

1 small red onion, sliced into rings

100 ml (3½ fl oz) skimmed milk

1 garlic clove, sliced

3 fresh thyme sprigs

2 tablespoons low fat soft cheese

salt and freshly ground black pepper

Serve with green beans and peas, tossed with 2 teaspoons of extra virgin olive oil.

1 Preheat the oven to Gas Mark 5/190°C/fan oven 170°C and place a baking tray in the oven.

2 Heat a non stick frying pan or griddle pan until hot and spray the steaks with the cooking spray. Cook in the pan for 1 minute on each side and then transfer to a plate. Set aside.

3 Put the potato, onion, milk, garlic and thyme in a lidded saucepan. Cover and cook gently for 10–15 minutes on a low heat until the potato is nearly tender. Strain, reserving all the cooking liquid and transfer the onion and potato to a bowl. Discard the thyme sprigs.

4 Mix the soft cheese with the reserved cooking liquid and season generously. Pour over the onion and potato and toss to coat. Leave to cool.

5 Carefully stack the onion and potato on top of each steak, remove the preheated baking tray from the oven and transfer the steaks to the baking tray. Bake for 15–20 minutes until the potato is golden. Sprinkle over some black pepper and serve immediately.

ⓥ **Variation...** For vegetarians, use the creamy potato and onion mixture to top two Quorn Quarter Pounder burgers as in step 5.

Honey mustard gammon with slow-roasted tomatoes

Serves 4

225 calories per serving

Takes 15 minutes to prepare
+ marinating, 1½ hours to
cook

**4 x 125 g (4½ oz) gammon
steaks, trimmed of visible fat**

2 teaspoons clear honey

**2 teaspoons wholegrain
mustard**

finely grated zest of an orange

**700 g (1 lb 9 oz) plum or vine
tomatoes**

**salt and freshly ground black
pepper**

*Slowly roasting the tomatoes intensifies their flavour, and
they're so delicious that you can eat them on toast or on
their own with a drizzle of balsamic vinegar.*

1 Arrange the gammon steaks in a shallow non metallic dish.
Mix together the honey, mustard and orange zest. Drizzle over
the gammon and leave to marinate for 1 hour, turning halfway
through.

2 Meanwhile, preheat the oven to Gas Mark 2/150°C/fan
oven 130°C. Cut the tomatoes in half and place cut side up
on a grill or cooling rack, resting on a baking tray. Season and
roast for 1½ hours.

3 Just before the tomatoes are ready, grill the gammon for
2–3 minutes on each side. Serve topped with the roasted
tomatoes.

Tip... You can cook up a double batch of tomatoes and keep
them in an airtight container in the fridge for up to 3 days.

Spring lamb pasta

Serves 4

480 calories per serving

Takes 20 minutes to prepare, 40 minutes to cook

An easy supper dish that combines spring lamb with spring vegetables in a tasty pasta meal. Use new season lamb if possible.

175 g (6 oz) dried pasta shapes

calorie controlled cooking spray

400 g (14 oz) lamb leg steaks, trimmed of visible fat and cubed

2 garlic cloves, chopped

leaves from 2 fresh rosemary sprigs

4 leeks, sliced

450 g (1 lb) carrots, peeled and sliced

175 g (6 oz) green beans

400 g can chopped tomatoes

500 ml (18 fl oz) lamb stock

125 g (4½ oz) mozzarella light, sliced thinly

salt and freshly ground black pepper

1 Preheat the oven to Gas Mark 6/200°C/fan oven 180°C.

2 Bring a pan of water to the boil, add the pasta and cook according to the packet instructions. Drain.

3 Spray a large non stick frying pan with the cooking spray and put over a medium heat. Add the lamb, garlic, rosemary and seasoning and brown the lamb all over.

4 Put the lamb in an ovenproof casserole dish and add all the other ingredients, including the pasta but except the mozzarella. Mix well. Lay the mozzarella slices on top and bake in the oven for 40 minutes.

Peppered steak with balsamic onions

Serves 2
421 calories per serving
Takes 30 minutes

500 g (1 lb 2 oz) potatoes, peeled and diced
½ beef stock cube
calorie controlled cooking spray
1 large onion, sliced thinly
2 tablespoons balsamic vinegar
1 tablespoon redcurrant jelly
2 x 110 g (4 oz) fillet or medallion steaks, trimmed of visible fat
salt and freshly ground black pepper

Try this mouth-watering recipe for a special occasion.

1 Preheat the oven to Gas Mark 7/220°C/fan oven 200°C. Bring a pan of water to the boil and add the potatoes and beef stock cube. Cook for 4 minutes and then drain, reserving the stock.

2 Tip the potatoes on to a non stick baking tray. Lightly spray with the cooking spray, spread out and cook in the oven for 20–25 minutes until crisp and golden.

3 Meanwhile, spray a lidded non stick pan with the cooking spray and fry the onion for 5 minutes over a high heat, until browned. Add the balsamic vinegar and 6 tablespoons of the reserved stock. Cover the pan and cook for 20 minutes until tender. Stir in the redcurrant jelly until melted.

4 Season the steaks generously with black pepper and a little salt. Fry in a non stick frying pan for 3–4 minutes on each side, or until done to your liking. Serve with the roasted potatoes and sticky onions.

Navarin of lamb

Serves 6

314 calories per serving

Takes 20 minutes to prepare,
2 hours to cook

❄

750 g (1 lb 10 oz) lean lamb
loin chops, trimmed of
visible fat and cut into
chunks

30 g (1¼ oz) plain white flour

calorie controlled cooking
spray

700 ml (1¼ pints) lamb or beef
stock

2 tablespoons tomato purée

2 onions, chopped

450 g (1 lb) baby carrots,
scrubbed

1 bouquet garni

18 sweet pickled small
silverskin onions, drained
and well rinsed

600 g (1 lb 5 oz) new potatoes,
scrubbed and halved if large

150 g (5½ oz) peas

salt and freshly ground black
pepper

2 tablespoons chopped fresh
parsley, to serve

*Baby vegetables give this casserole a delicious spring
flavour.*

1 Preheat the oven to Gas Mark 4/180°C/fan oven 160°C.

2 Roll the meat in the flour and season well. Heat a large,
lidded, flameproof and ovenproof casserole dish, spray with the
cooking spray and brown the meat all over.

3 Mix any remaining flour into the stock with the tomato purée
and pour it over the meat. Add the chopped onions, carrots and
bouquet garni and bring to the boil. Cover and cook in the oven
for 1¼ hours.

4 Add the silverskin onions, potatoes and peas and cook for a
further 45 minutes or until the vegetables are cooked. Remove
the bouquet garni and serve sprinkled with the parsley.

Tip... If you don't have a pan that you can use both on
the hob and in the oven, use a large frying pan and then
transfer the meat to an ovenproof casserole dish.

Stuffed pork loin

Serves 4
350 calories per serving
Takes 40 minutes to prepare,
1½ hours to cook

600 g (1 lb 5 oz) lean pork loin
joint, fat trimmed to a thin
layer

grated zest and juice of ½ a
lemon

30 g (1¼ oz) dried bulgur
wheat

calorie controlled cooking
spray

2 shallots, chopped finely

1 small eating apple, cored
and diced

8 fresh sage leaves, chopped

7 stoned black olives in brine,
drained and chopped finely

3 tablespoons low fat soft
cheese

salt and freshly ground black
pepper

*Serve with carrots, cauliflower, peas and potatoes roasted
in 2 teaspoons of sunflower oil.*

1 Preheat the oven to Gas Mark 5/190°C/fan oven 170°C. Put
the pork on a board, with the fat at the top. Cut the pork about
1 cm (½ inch) below the top of the pork lengthways, then turn
the knife and cut around in a spiral, eventually enabling you to
roll the meat out flat. Put the pork in a shallow dish, cut side up
and sprinkle with the lemon zest and lemon juice. Set aside.

2 To make the stuffing, bring a pan of water to the boil, add
the bulgur wheat and simmer for 15 minutes until tender.
Drain.

3 Meanwhile, heat a non stick frying pan and spray with
the cooking spray. Cook the shallots, apple and sage for
5–8 minutes until softened. Put into a bowl. Stir in the bulgur
wheat, olives and soft cheese and season. Set aside to cool.

4 Spoon the stuffing along the length of the pork. Re-roll
the pork and tie with kitchen string in about 5 places. If any
stuffing comes out, squidge it back in.

5 Place in a non stick roasting tin, cover with foil and roast
for 45 minutes. Remove the foil and roast for a further
30–40 minutes or until cooked. Carve into thick slices and
serve.

Fantastic fish and seafood

Summery prawn pasta

Serves 2
363 calories per serving
Takes 15 minutes

125 g (4½ oz) dried pasta
shells
150 g (5½ oz) broccoli, cut
into small florets
150 g (5½ oz) sugar snap
peas, halved
calorie controlled cooking
spray
1 garlic clove, crushed
4 ripe tomatoes, chopped
roughly
grated zest and juice of a
small lemon
200 g (7 oz) cooked peeled
prawns, defrosted if frozen
salt and freshly ground black
pepper

*A zingy, fresh tasting pasta recipe that's packed full of
colour – and tastes great.*

1 Bring a pan of water to the boil, add the pasta and cook for
10–12 minutes, or according to the packet instructions. Add
the broccoli and sugar snap peas for the last 3 minutes of the
cooking time.

2 Meanwhile, lightly spray a non stick saucepan with the
cooking spray, add the garlic and fry for 30 seconds without
browning.

3 Stir in the tomatoes, lemon zest, lemon juice and seasoning
and cook for 2–3 minutes until the tomatoes have softened
slightly. Stir in the prawns and heat through for 1 minute. Drain
the pasta and vegetables and toss together with the prawns
and vegetables. Serve immediately.

Crispy salmon on creamy greens

Serves 2
291 calories per serving
Takes 15 minutes

½ teaspoon cayenne pepper

2 x 125 g (4½ oz) skinless salmon fillets

calorie controlled cooking spray

1 courgette

1 garlic clove, sliced

100 g (3½ oz) baby spinach, washed

75 g (2¾ oz) low fat soft cheese

15 g (½ oz) capers in brine, drained and rinsed

2 tablespoons finely chopped fresh flat leaf parsley

grated zest of ½ a lemon, plus wedges to serve

salt and freshly ground black pepper

Sprinkling spice on to skinless salmon before cooking gives the fish a crunchy crust. Serve with 150 g (5½ oz) diced potatoes per person, sautéed in calorie controlled cooking spray, and baby carrots.

1 Put the cayenne pepper on to a plate and dip in each salmon fillet, pressing down gently to coat one side. Heat a non stick frying pan until hot and spray the salmon with the cooking spray. Cook for 3 minutes, pepper side down, and then flip over and cook for 2 minutes. Remove from the heat, wrap the salmon in foil and set aside.

2 Meanwhile, using a potato peeler, cut the courgette into ribbons. Spray the frying pan again with the cooking spray and cook the garlic, courgette ribbons and spinach for 2 minutes. Stir in the soft cheese and 3 tablespoons of cold water until smooth and the spinach is wilted.

3 Remove from the heat and stir through the capers, parsley, lemon zest and seasoning. Unwrap the salmon and serve immediately with the wilted creamy greens and lemon wedges.

Trout stuffed with couscous, almonds and herbs

Serves 4

450 calories per serving

Takes 25 minutes to prepare,
15–20 minutes to cook

**calorie controlled cooking
  spray**

1 small onion, chopped finely

2 garlic cloves, crushed

1 teaspoon ground cumin

100 g (3½ oz) dried couscous

**300 ml (10 fl oz) vegetable
  stock**

**1 tablespoon chopped fresh
  parsley**

**2 tablespoons chopped fresh
  mint**

**4 x 200 g (7 oz) whole trout,
  heads removed and boned**

**40 g (1½ oz) flaked almonds,
  chopped**

**salt and freshly ground black
  pepper**

*A very impressive Moroccan-inspired dish, where the
couscous and spices are cooked inside the fish. Serve with
a fresh, light salad.*

1 Preheat the oven to Gas Mark 6/200°C/fan oven 180°C.

2 Heat a non stick frying pan and spray with the cooking
spray. Fry the onion for 2–3 minutes, until softened. Add the
garlic and cumin and cook for 1 minute more.

3 Add the couscous, vegetable stock and herbs and stir
well. Bring to the boil, remove from the heat and leave for
10–15 minutes, to allow the couscous to absorb the stock.

4 Season the trout and fill each one with the couscous. Place
the fish in a shallow ovenproof dish that has been sprayed
with the cooking spray. Sprinkle with the chopped almonds.

5 Bake in the oven for 15–20 minutes until the fish is tender.

Soy prawns on courgette cakes

Serves 4

240 calories per serving

Takes 20 minutes to prepare,
 20 minutes to cook

1 teaspoon sunflower oil

12 peeled cooked king
 prawns, defrosted if frozen

2 tablespoons dark soy sauce

1 tablespoon medium sherry

1 teaspoon clear honey

½ teaspoon sesame oil

1 teaspoon sesame seeds

For the courgette cakes

450 g (1 lb) courgettes, grated
 coarsely

1 egg, beaten

50 g (1¾ oz) dried polenta

1 tablespoon sunflower oil

salt and freshly ground black
 pepper

*Choose large plump king prawns; they are expensive but
well worth it for special occasions.*

1 To make the cakes, place the grated courgettes in a
mixing bowl with the egg and polenta. Season well and mix
thoroughly.

2 You will need to cook the courgette cakes in batches. To do
this, heat half the oil in a large non stick frying pan and drop
spoonfuls of the mixture into the pan, pressing down with the
back of a spoon. Cook over a low heat for about 5 minutes
per side until golden and crisp. Continue with the remaining
mixture. Keep the cooked cakes warm while you prepare the
prawns.

3 Heat a griddle pan or heavy based pan and wipe with the
sunflower oil. Add the prawns and cook over a high heat for
1–2 minutes on each side until hot, depending on how large
they are. Mix together the soy sauce, sherry and honey and add
to the pan. Allow the juices to bubble for a few seconds. Drizzle
with the sesame oil and scatter with the seeds. Toss briefly.

4 Serve the prawns on the courgette cakes and drizzle with
any remaining pan juices.

Mediterranean sardines

Serves 4
334 calories per serving
Takes 25 minutes

calorie controlled cooking
 spray
3 garlic cloves, crushed
2 shallots, chopped finely
1 red chilli, de-seeded and
 chopped finely
a small bunch of fresh
 coriander, chopped
8 x 100 g (3½ oz) very fresh
 sardines, cleaned, flattened
 out and the backbone
 removed (see Tip)
salt and freshly ground black
 pepper

To serve
1 lemon, halved
a bunch of fresh parsley or
 coriander, chopped

Serve these delicious sardines with a large mixed salad.

1 Soak eight cocktail sticks in water for 10 minutes to prevent them from burning under the grill. Heat a non stick frying pan, spray with the cooking spray and add the garlic and shallots. Cook for a few minutes with 2 tablespoons of water and then add the chilli, coriander and seasoning.

2 Spread this mixture over the flesh side of the sardines, roll them up from head to tail and secure with a cocktail stick. Cook under a hot grill for 3–4 minutes, turning once or twice, until they are cooked through. Squeeze over the lemon, scatter over the parsley or coriander and serve.

Tip... To remove the bones from a sardine, first remove the head then slit along its belly and remove the guts. Lay the sardine on a board, slit side down, skin side up, with the two sides opened out. Gently press down on the backbone through the skin until you feel it give. Do this all along the length of the back and then turn the fish up the other way and gently pull out the backbone. It should come away easily, bringing the attached bones with it. Any individual bones that are left can be removed with your fingers. Wash the fish well and it is ready for cooking.

Salmon strudel

Serves 4

320 calories per serving

Takes 25 minutes to prepare
+ 20 minutes cooling,
40 minutes to cook

1 courgette, sliced

2 red peppers, quartered and de-seeded

1 red onion, cut into thin wedges

2 tablespoons balsamic vinegar

calorie controlled cooking spray

8 x 15 g (¼ oz) sheets filo pastry, measuring 30 x 40 cm (12 x 16 inches)

3 x 125 g (4½ oz) skinless salmon fillets, halved horizontally to make 6 thin fillets

2 tablespoons low fat soft cheese with garlic and herbs

salt and freshly ground black pepper

Serve with 100 g (3½ oz) boiled new potatoes per person, mange tout and carrots.

1 Preheat the oven to Gas Mark 6/200°C/fan oven 180°C. Put the courgette slices, peppers and onion on a non stick baking tray, drizzle with the balsamic vinegar and spray with the cooking spray. Season and roast in the oven for 20 minutes until starting to char a little. Leave to cool for 20 minutes.

2 Lay two sheets of filo pastry on a non stick baking tray, slightly overlapping to make a square. Spray with the cooking spray and lay another 2 sheets over the top. Repeat once more.

3 Lay the thin salmon fillets down the centre of the square, leaving a 2.5 cm (1 inch) border at either end. Season with black pepper and spread the soft cheese over the fillets. Arrange the cooled vegetables on top.

4 Spray the exposed filo pastry with the cooking spray and fold the pastry up and over to enclose the salmon completely, sealing the ends. Spray again with the cooking spray and crumple the remaining filo sheets over the top. Spray once more with the cooking spray and bake in the oven for 20 minutes until golden and cooked.

Belgian mussels

Serves 2
335 calories per serving
Takes 30 minutes

1 garlic clove, chopped
100 ml (3½ fl oz) white wine
600 g (1lb 5 oz) fresh mussels, prepared (see Tip)
4 spring onions, sliced finely
2 tablespoons double cream
salt and freshly ground black pepper

To serve

1 tablespoon finely chopped fresh flat leaf parsley
1 tablespoon finely chopped fresh dill

Serve with a 50 g (1¾ oz) bread roll per person and a mixed salad drizzled with balsamic vinegar.

1 Put the garlic, wine and 100 ml (3½ fl oz) of water into a large lidded pan and bring to the boil. Cover and simmer for 5 minutes. Add the mussels and quickly replace the lid. Cook for 3–4 minutes, occasionally shaking the pan. Check that the mussels have opened. If not, cook for 1 minute more.

2 Remove the mussels and place in two large bowls, discarding any closed mussels. Cover each bowl with foil to keep warm.

3 Add the spring onions and cream to the pan and bubble for a few minutes until thickened. Season. Remove the foil and pour the cream sauce over the mussels. Scatter with the parsley and dill to serve.

Tip... To prepare mussels, scrub off any dirt and remove any barnacles. Remove the beard, if any, that sticks out between the shells. Discard any mussels that are already open or have a cracked shell.

Chilli and tomato salsa pollack

Serves 2
411 calories per serving
Takes 25 minutes

½ a kettleful of boiling water

125 g (4½ oz) dried long grain rice

25 g (1 oz) fresh root ginger, chopped

2 garlic cloves, chopped

1 large chilli, de-seeded and chopped

2 tomatoes, chopped

1 tablespoon red wine vinegar

2 teaspoons caster sugar

calorie controlled cooking spray

250 g (9 oz) skinless thick pollack fillet, cut into chunks

½ x 25 g packet fresh coriander, chopped

salt and freshly ground black pepper

This fragrant dish is delicious served with a simple cucumber salad, mixed with chopped Little Gem lettuce.

1 Put the boiling water in a saucepan and bring back to the boil. Add the rice and cook for 15 minutes until tender. Drain and return to the pan.

2 Meanwhile, in a food processor or with a hand blender, whizz the ginger, garlic, chilli, tomatoes, vinegar and sugar to a coarse purée. Set aside.

3 Heat a lidded non stick frying pan and spray with the cooking spray. Cook the pollack chunks for 3 minutes, stirring until lightly browned. Remove from the pan and set aside.

4 Pour the chilli salsa into the frying pan and bubble for 2 minutes until thick and deep red. Return the pollack to the frying pan, cover and remove from the heat. Set aside until the rice is cooked.

5 Stir the coriander and seasoning into the rice and serve with the pollack.

Braised sea bass with fresh tomato sauce

Serves 4

300 calories per serving

Takes 10 minutes to prepare,
25 minutes to cook

450 g (1 lb) new potatoes,
scrubbed

calorie controlled cooking
spray

1 onion, chopped

2 garlic cloves, crushed

450 g (1 lb) vine ripened
tomatoes, chopped

1 tablespoon tomato purée

½ vegetable stock cube,
crumbled

50 ml (2 fl oz) white wine

60 g (2 oz) stoned black olives
in brine, drained and sliced

a handful of fresh basil leaves,
plus extra to garnish

8 x 75 g (2¾ oz) sea bass
fillets

salt and freshly ground black
pepper

Full of Mediterranean flavours, this is a great dish for a midweek meal.

1 Preheat the oven to Gas Mark 5/190°C/fan oven 170°C. Bring a pan of water to the boil, add the potatoes and cook for 15 minutes or until tender. Drain.

2 Meanwhile, spray a lidded non stick saucepan with the cooking spray and heat until hot. Add the onion and cook, stirring, for 3 minutes until beginning to soften. Add the garlic and cook for a further minute. Add the tomatoes, tomato purée, stock cube, wine and 50 ml (2 fl oz) of water. Bring to the boil, cover, reduce the heat and simmer for 10 minutes until soft. Stir in the olives and basil.

3 Spoon the sauce into an ovenproof dish. Season the fish on both sides and lay on top of the sauce. Bake for 10 minutes until the fish just flakes.

4 Serve the fish with the sauce spooned over, scattered with the extra basil leaves and with the potatoes on the side.

Variation... Try this recipe with the same amount of mackerel fillets, in place of the sea bass.

Thai steamed salmon

Serves 2
320 calories per serving
Takes 30 minutes

Steaming times for fish are totally dependent on the thickness rather than the weight, so measure your fish carefully. This Thai-influenced recipe is light yet flavoursome.

calorie controlled cooking spray

4 shallots, sliced finely

2.5 cm (1 inch) fresh root ginger, sliced into fine matchsticks

2 garlic cloves, sliced into fine slivers

25 g (1 oz) light brown soft sugar

2 tablespoons fish sauce

2 x 150 g (5½ oz) salmon steaks, each about 3 cm (1¼ inches) thick

a few fresh coriander sprigs, to garnish

1 Heat a non stick frying pan and spray with the cooking spray. Fry the shallots, ginger and garlic for 1 minute until aromatic and then add the sugar and fish sauce. Stir and set aside.

2 Place each piece of salmon in the middle of a piece of non stick baking parchment, at least four times its size. Pile the ginger mixture on top of each and then fold up the baking parchment around the fish to make an airtight parcel.

3 Place both parcels in a steamer, cover and steam for 10 minutes or until the steaks are opaque and cooked through. Serve immediately with the juices poured over and fresh coriander sprigs to garnish.

Tip... Steam fish either in a fish kettle, bamboo steamer or saucepan with a steaming basket.

Prawns with lime and chillies

Serves 4
100 calories per serving
Takes 20 minutes

calorie controlled cooking
  spray
2 onions, sliced
1 large green pepper,
  de-seeded and sliced
2 courgettes, sliced diagonally
1 tablespoon mustard seeds
2 teaspoons fennel seeds
1 long red chilli, de-seeded
  and sliced thinly
2 garlic cloves, chopped finely
250 g (9 oz) cooked peeled
  tiger prawns, defrosted if
  frozen
juice of a lime
salt and freshly ground black
  pepper
2 tablespoons chopped fresh
  coriander, to garnish

A very simple but stunning dish.

1 Spray a large, lidded, non stick frying pan with the cooking spray and stir-fry the onions over a medium heat for 7 minutes until softened.

2 Re-spray the pan if necessary and toss in the green pepper, courgettes, mustard seeds, fennel seeds, chilli and garlic. Stir-fry for 2 minutes.

3 Add the prawns, lime juice and 125 ml (4 fl oz) of water, stir, cover and simmer over a low heat for 2 minutes. Season and serve sprinkled with the coriander.

Skate with capers and garlic

Serves 2
190 calories per serving
Takes 15 minutes

2 x 225 g (8 oz) skate wings
1 bay leaf
6 peppercorns
a fresh parsley sprig
a kettleful of boiling water

For the sauce
1 garlic clove, sliced into fine slivers
1 tablespoon olive oil
2 tablespoons white wine vinegar
2 tablespoons capers, drained
2 tablespoons chopped fresh parsley

If you have not eaten skate before then do try it – it is easy to cook, has no bones, is delicately flavoured and has a meaty texture. Serve with 200 g (7 oz) cooked new potatoes per person and steamed spinach or broccoli.

1 Put the skate wings in a large frying pan with the bay leaf, peppercorns and parsley. Pour in boiling water to cover and bring back to the boil. Simmer for 6 minutes until the fish is cooked through and then drain.

2 In a separate non stick pan, fry the garlic in the olive oil until just golden and then carefully add the vinegar (the oil may spit). Add the capers and parsley and stir in.

3 To serve, place the skate on warmed plates and pour the sauce over.

Variation... Skate is also very good grilled under a medium heat for 3–4 minutes on each side and then served with this sauce.

Tandoori-style prawns

Serves 2

121 calories per serving

Takes 20 minutes

200 g (7 oz) peeled raw tiger prawns, defrosted if frozen

1 tablespoon tandoori curry powder

1 tablespoon low fat natural yogurt

juice of ½ a lemon

¼ cucumber, halved, de-seeded and sliced finely into crescents

½ x 25 g packet fresh coriander, chopped

8 cherry tomatoes, halved

1 teaspoon fish sauce

15 g (½ oz) pickled sushi ginger, shredded, plus 2 tablespoons juice reserved from the jar

1 Little Gem lettuce, shredded finely

Enjoyed hot or cold, this is a great way to add a little bit of spice to a midweek supper. Serve with a 225 g (8 oz) potato per person, baked in its skin.

1 Using a small knife, carefully score a shallow cut along the back of each prawn from the top to the tail. Put in a bowl along with the tandoori curry powder, yogurt and lemon juice. Stir to coat in the marinade.

2 Preheat the grill to high. Meanwhile, make the salad. In another bowl, mix together the cucumber, coriander, cherry tomatoes, fish sauce, ginger and its juice and lettuce. Set aside.

3 Put the prawns on a foil-lined tray and grill for 5 minutes, turning halfway until cooked. Serve immediately with the salad.

Trout parcels

Serves 2

177 calories per serving

Takes 20 minutes to prepare,
25 minutes to cook

calorie controlled cooking spray

50 g (1¾ oz) fennel bulb, diced finely

1 carrot, peeled and cut into very thin strips

2 tablespoons chopped fresh parsley

1 tomato, peeled and diced

50 ml (2 fl oz) fish or vegetable stock

2 x 225 g (8 oz) whole trout, heads on (see Tip)

1 lemon slice, halved

salt and freshly ground black pepper

Fennel goes beautifully with trout in this simple recipe.

1 Preheat the oven to Gas Mark 4/180°C/fan oven 160°C.

2 Spray a small non stick pan with the cooking spray. Add the fennel and carrot and cook for 5 minutes. Stir in the parsley, tomato, stock and seasoning. Let it sizzle for a few minutes until almost all the liquid has evaporated.

3 Cut two large pieces of foil. Put a trout in the centre of each one and use the vegetable mixture to stuff the trout. Don't worry if it won't all fit in, it will still cook if left alongside the fish. Finally, push a half lemon slice inside each trout and seal the foil into a parcel.

4 Place in an ovenproof dish and bake in the oven for 25 minutes.

5 Open one of the trout parcels to check if the fish is cooked – the eyes will have turned white and the flesh will flake easily. To serve, re-seal the parcel, allowing the aromatic steam to escape when opened.

Tip... Leaving the heads on makes it easier to judge when the fish is cooked. If you prefer to serve the fish without the heads, remove them once you've checked the fish is cooked.

Simply vegetarian

Butternut squash and goat's cheese strudel

Serves 4

284 calories per serving

Takes 40 minutes to prepare,
15 minutes to cook

600 g (1lb 5 oz) butternut
squash, peeled, de-seeded
and diced

1 red pepper, de-seeded and
cut into 1 cm (½ inch) dice

calorie controlled cooking
spray

1 large leek, sliced

25 g (1 oz) pecans, chopped
roughly

6 x 45 g (1½ oz) sheets filo
pastry, measuring
50 x 24 cm (20 x 9½ inches)

100 g (3½ oz) soft rinded
goat's cheese, diced

salt and freshly ground black
pepper

To serve

150 g (5½ oz) 0% fat Greek
yogurt

1 small garlic clove, crushed

1 tablespoon snipped fresh
chives

Just the thing for a smart vegetarian main course.

1 Preheat the oven to Gas Mark 7/220°C/fan oven 200°C.
Mix together the squash and red pepper, spread out on a
large non stick baking tray, lightly spray with the cooking
spray, season and roast for 10 minutes.

2 Stir the leek into the vegetables and cook for 5 minutes, then
add the pecans and cook for another 5 minutes. Remove and
cool slightly.

3 Cut the sheets of filo pastry in half to give 12 smaller
squares. For each strudel, layer up three of these pieces, lightly
spraying with the cooking spray between each layer. Spoon a
quarter of the vegetables on to each pastry square and divide
the goat's cheese between them.

4 Roll each square up into a log, tucking in the ends to hold
in the filling. Transfer to a baking tray, lightly mist with the
cooking spray and bake for 15 minutes until crisp.

5 Mix the yogurt with the garlic, chives and seasoning and
serve with the strudels.

Zesty veggie fried rice

Serves 2
361 calories per serving
Takes 40 minutes

125 g (4½ oz) dried brown basmati rice

calorie controlled cooking spray

25 g (1 oz) cashews, chopped

1 courgette, diced

150 g (5½ oz) mushrooms, sliced

6 spring onions, sliced

1 teaspoon grated fresh root ginger

1 garlic clove, crushed

1 red chilli, de-seeded and chopped

100 g (3½ oz) frozen peas

finely grated zest and juice of ½ a lemon

The delicious combination of lemon, ginger and chilli gives this colourful stir-fry a fresh and zingy flavour. Cashew nuts add a welcome crunch.

1 Bring a pan of water to the boil, add the rice and cook for 25 minutes or according to the packet instructions.

2 After about 20 minutes, heat a wok or large non stick frying pan until hot and spray with the cooking spray. Stir-fry the cashews until golden brown and then tip into a small bowl.

3 Add the courgette and mushrooms to the wok or frying pan and stir-fry for 3–4 minutes before adding the spring onions, ginger, garlic and chilli. Cook for 1 minute, stirring. Mix in the frozen peas and cook for 1 minute more.

4 Drain the rice and rinse in cold water. Drain again. Add to the wok or frying pan with the lemon zest and juice. Stir-fry for 2 minutes or until piping hot and then serve in warmed bowls, topped with the cashew nuts.

Tip... Brown rice takes a little longer to cook than white rice. However, you can make life much easier by cooking several portions of rice at once. Spread out the drained, cooked rice in a large shallow dish to cool and then freeze individual portions weighing 150 g (5½ oz).

Variation... Why not try ringing the changes by swapping the vegetables in the recipe for other vegetables such as peppers, baby corn and mange tout?

Penne with watercress sauce

Serves 2
234 calories per serving
Takes 20 minutes

110 g (4 oz) dried penne
calorie controlled cooking
  spray
2 garlic cloves, crushed
200 g bag watercress, thick
  stalks removed
2 teaspoons balsamic vinegar
2 tomatoes, de-seeded and
  diced
salt and freshly ground black
  pepper
2 tablespoons snipped fresh
  chives, to garnish

Whizz up this vibrant meal in just a few minutes.

1 Bring a large pan of water to the boil, add the pasta and cook for 10–12 minutes or according to the packet instructions. Drain and rinse thoroughly.

2 Meanwhile, heat a large non stick pan and spray with the cooking spray. Add the garlic and cook over a medium heat for 2 minutes and then add the watercress and cook for 1–2 minutes until just wilted. Transfer to a food processor or blender, add the balsamic vinegar and 1 tablespoon of hot water and whizz for 1 minute until smooth.

3 Return to the pan with the pasta, add the tomatoes and toss to mix. Season and serve garnished with the chives.

Variation... For a non-vegetarian version, mix a 165 g (5¾ oz) cooked, sliced, skinless chicken breast into the sauce.

Honey mustard Quorn fillets with baby vegetables

Serves 4
234 calories per serving
Takes 25 minutes

400 g (14 oz) small new
  potatoes, scrubbed and
  halved
150 g (5½ oz) Chantenay
  carrots, scrubbed and
  trimmed
150 g (5½ oz) baby corn,
  halved
100 g (3½ oz) sugar snap peas
calorie controlled cooking
  spray
8 frozen Quorn Fillets
juice of a lemon
2 tablespoons wholegrain
  mustard
4 rounded teaspoons clear
  honey

Pretty as a picture with its medley of baby vegetables, this is a most attractive vegetarian main course.

1 Bring a large lidded saucepan of water to the boil, add the new potatoes, cover and cook for 10 minutes. Add the carrots, cover and cook for 5 minutes and then finally add the baby corn and sugar snap peas. Cover and cook for 4 minutes more and then drain all the vegetables.

2 Meanwhile, heat a large, lidded, non stick frying pan until hot and spray with the cooking spray. Brown the Quorn fillets for 5–6 minutes over a high heat, turning to colour evenly. Reduce the heat and add the lemon juice, mustard and honey plus 2 tablespoons of water. Cover the pan and simmer gently for 8 minutes.

3 Push the Quorn fillets to the side of the pan, add the drained vegetables and toss through the sauce. Serve the Quorn on a bed of the glazed vegetables.

Variation... For a non-vegetarian version, try this recipe with four 125 g (4½ oz) skinless chicken breast fillets instead of the Quorn. Brown the chicken for 8–10 minutes before adding the sauce in step 2.

Balsamic roasted red onion pizza with feta

Serves 2

396 calories per serving

Takes 10 minutes to prepare,
45 minutes to cook

23 cm (9 inch) ready-made
thin and crispy pizza base

For the topping

3 red onions, each cut into
6 wedges

calorie controlled cooking
spray

4 tablespoons balsamic
vinegar

3 or 4 bushy fresh thyme
sprigs, plus extra to garnish

400 g can chopped tomatoes

1 garlic clove, crushed

75 g (2¾ oz) reduced fat feta
cheese, crumbled

salt and freshly ground black
pepper

*Sweet roasted onions and sharp feta cheese turn a simple
pizza into something special.*

1 Preheat the oven to Gas Mark 6/200°C/fan oven 180°C.
Spread the onion wedges evenly over the base of a large non
stick roasting tin. Spray with the cooking spray and drizzle over
the balsamic vinegar and 5 tablespoons of water. Scatter
over the thyme sprigs and transfer to the oven. Roast for
30 minutes, stirring once or twice, until the onions are tender
and the balsamic vinegar and water have been reduced to a
sticky coating.

2 Meanwhile, put the tomatoes and garlic in a saucepan and
bring to the boil. Season and simmer for 20–25 minutes until
thickened.

3 Warm a non stick baking tray in the oven for 2–3 minutes.
Remove and spray with the cooking spray. Put the pizza base
on the tray and spread over the tomato sauce. Top with the
roasted onions (discarding the thyme sprigs) and scatter over
the feta cheese. Bake for 12–15 minutes until the pizza base
and cheese are golden. Serve immediately, scattered with a
little extra fresh thyme.

Moroccan stew with green herb couscous

Serves 4
350 calories per serving
Takes 15 minutes to prepare, 20 minutes to cook ✔ ❄ (freeze stew and couscous separately)

Vegetable and bean stews are quick to make and tasty for vegetarians and meat eaters alike. Couscous makes a great storecupboard stand by and is very easy to prepare.

1 large onion, chopped
1 carrot, peeled and sliced thinly
2 teaspoons garlic purée
1 tablespoon ginger purée or grated fresh root ginger (optional)
1 large green chilli, de-seeded and chopped
2 teaspoons olive oil
1 teaspoon ground cumin
2 teaspoons ground coriander
1 teaspoon paprika
¼ teaspoon ground cinnamon
a good pinch of saffron strands or ¼ teaspoon turmeric (optional)

400 g can chopped tomatoes
1 courgette, chopped
400 g can chick peas, drained and liquid reserved
salt and freshly ground black pepper

For the couscous
200 g (7 oz) dried couscous
400 ml (14 fl oz) boiling water
1 teaspoon extra virgin olive oil
2 tablespoons chopped fresh parsley
1 tablespoon chopped fresh dill or coriander

1 To make the couscous, put it in a big bowl and pour over the boiling water. Add the olive oil and black pepper to taste. Stir well and allow to cool, stirring occasionally with a fork to separate the grains.

2 For the stew, put the onion, carrot, garlic purée, ginger (if using) and chilli in a large lidded saucepan with the oil and 4 tablespoons of water. Heat until it all starts to sizzle and then cover the pan and simmer for 10 minutes.

continues opposite ▶

3 Stir in the cumin, coriander, paprika, cinnamon and saffron or turmeric, if using. Cook for 1 minute. Add the tomatoes, courgette, chick peas with the reserved liquid and seasoning. Bring to the boil and simmer for about 5 minutes until the courgette is tender.

4 Meanwhile, cover the couscous and reheat it in the microwave on high for 5 minutes. Alternatively, preheat the oven to Gas Mark 4/180°C/fan oven 160°C, place the couscous in an ovenproof dish, covered with foil, and heat for 10 minutes. When the couscous is piping hot, stir in the chopped herbs.

5 Serve the couscous with the stew spooned on top.

Sausages with peppers and lentils

Serves 4

237 calories per serving

Takes 20 minutes to prepare,
20 minutes to cook

8 vegetarian sausages

calorie controlled cooking
spray

1 onion, sliced thinly

1 large leek, sliced

1 large red pepper, de-seeded
and chopped

1 large yellow or orange
pepper, de-seeded and
chopped

1 carrot, peeled and sliced
thinly

100 g (3½ oz) mushrooms,
halved

300 ml (10 fl oz) vegetable
stock

2 tablespoons sun-dried
tomato purée

1 tablespoon chopped fresh
rosemary or 2 teaspoons
dried rosemary

410 g can green lentils,
drained and rinsed

freshly ground black pepper

This is comfort food at its best.

1 Preheat the oven to Gas Mark 5/190°C/fan oven 170°C.

2 Put the sausages in a large ovenproof baking or casserole dish and set to one side.

3 Heat a large non stick frying pan or wok and spray with the cooking spray. Add the onion, leek, peppers, carrot and mushrooms. Stir-fry them for 5–6 minutes, until softened. Tip them into the baking or casserole dish.

4 Pour the stock into the baking or casserole dish and add the tomato purée, rosemary and lentils. Mix well and season with black pepper.

5 Transfer the baking or casserole dish to the oven and bake for 20 minutes, uncovered. Serve.

Variation... For a non-vegetarian version, use the same number of Weight Watchers Premium Pork sausages instead of the vegetarian ones. You'll need to brown them under the grill before adding the remaining ingredients.

Warming vegetable pilau

Serves 4
315 calories per serving
Takes 22 minutes

calorie controlled cooking
   spray
1 courgette, cut into small
   chunks
1 red pepper, de-seeded and
   cut into small pieces
1 tablespoon pilau rice
   seasoning
250 g (9 oz) dried Arborio rice
125 ml (4 fl oz) dry white wine
600 ml (20 fl oz) hot vegetable
   stock
100 g (3½ oz) cherry
   tomatoes, halved
100 g (3½ oz) sugar snap peas
25 g (1 oz) toasted flaked
   almonds

A twist on the Indian classic using Arborio rice for a truly satisfying dinner. You can use your favourite veggies or whatever you have in the fridge.

1 Heat a large, lidded, non stick saucepan and spray with the cooking spray. Cook the courgette and pepper for 3 minutes until starting to colour, stirring occasionally. Stir in the pilau rice seasoning and Arborio rice until coated in the spices. Add the white wine and allow it to bubble for 30 seconds.

2 Gradually add half the vegetable stock, stirring between additions until the rice is sticking to the base of the pan. Add the remaining stock, cover and simmer for 7 minutes, stirring halfway.

3 Scatter over the cherry tomatoes and sugar snap peas. Cover and cook for a further 3 minutes until tender and most of the liquid has been absorbed. Do not stir. Scatter over the almonds, stir and serve immediately.

Tip... This serves 8 as a side dish.

Caramelised onion and polenta slice

Serves 8

143 calories per serving

Takes 20 minutes to prepare,
50 minutes to cook

200 g (7 oz) dried polenta

calorie controlled cooking spray

1 kg (2 lb 4 oz) onions, sliced finely

a small bunch of fresh marjoram, oregano or parsley, chopped

4 large beefsteak tomatoes, sliced

salt and freshly ground black pepper

Polenta is a great dish to serve with stews, meat or ragu sauces.

1 Cook the polenta according to the packet instructions. Pour into a 20 cm (8 inch) deep springform cake tin and set aside to cool.

2 Heat a large non stick frying pan and spray with the cooking spray. Add the onions and stir-fry for a few minutes before turning the heat to low and covering the onions with a sheet of non stick baking parchment and a lid. Cook the onions like this for 30 minutes, until soft and caramelised, stirring occasionally to ensure that they don't burn. Preheat the oven to Gas Mark 4/180°C/fan oven 160°C.

3 Sprinkle the herbs over the polenta, reserving some to garnish, tip in the onions and spread them over the top. Top with the tomatoes and season. Bake for 20 minutes.

4 Remove from the tin, scatter with the reserved herbs and cut into eight slices to serve.

Tip... To prepare polenta, place one part polenta grain to three parts boiling water in a pan. Cover and leave to cook for up to 40 minutes until light and fluffy. Stir occasionally during the cooking to give the grain plenty of air.

Falafel with cucumber salsa

Serves 4

145 calories per serving

Takes 20 minutes to prepare,
15 minutes to cook

❅ (falafel only)

**410 g can chick peas, drained
and rinsed**

1 garlic clove, crushed

**50 g (1¾ oz) wholemeal
breadcrumbs**

4 spring onions, sliced thinly

1 egg

1 teaspoon ground cumin

**calorie controlled cooking
spray**

**salt and freshly ground black
pepper**

**½ Iceberg lettuce, shredded,
to serve**

For the salsa

**175 g (6 oz) cucumber, diced
finely**

**3 tablespoons chopped fresh
coriander**

1 tablespoon mint jelly

**150 g (5½ oz) low fat natural
yogurt**

Tasty falafel go beautifully with a cool cucumber salsa.

1 Preheat the oven to Gas Mark 5/190°C/fan oven 170°C.

2 To make the falafel, place the chick peas, garlic, breadcrumbs, spring onions, egg, cumin and seasoning in a food processor and whizz until smooth. If you don't have a food processor, mash the ingredients together thoroughly.

3 Line a baking tray with non stick baking parchment. Using wet hands, shape the chick pea mixture into 20 small balls. Place them on the prepared baking tray and spray them lightly with the cooking spray. Bake for 15 minutes.

4 Meanwhile, make the salsa. Mix together the cucumber, coriander, mint jelly and yogurt and spoon this into four small dishes. Serve five falafel each, hot or cold, on a bed of shredded lettuce, with the salsa for dipping.

Variation... For a more substantial meal, split a warmed medium pitta bread and stuff it with the cooked falafel and lettuce. Drizzle the filled pitta bread with the salsa.

Seared vegetable spiralini

Serves 2
430 calories per serving
Takes 30 minutes

110 g (4 oz) dried spiralini

300 g (10½ oz) butternut squash, peeled and cut into small slices

1 small red onion, cut into wedges

1 yellow pepper, de-seeded and cut into wedges

calorie controlled cooking spray

8 fresh sage leaves

410 g can butter beans, drained and rinsed

2 tablespoons balsamic vinegar

salt and freshly ground black pepper

A simple dish, searing the vegetables adds a touch of extra flavour.

1 Bring a large pan of water to the boil, add the pasta and cook according to the packet instructions. Drain and keep warm.

2 Heat a griddle pan or non stick frying pan until hot. Spray the vegetables with the cooking spray and cook in batches until charred and just tender. Add the sage leaves to wilt.

3 Toss all the vegetables together with the pasta, butter beans and balsamic vinegar. Season before serving warm.

Stuffed baby squash

Serves 4

316 calories per serving

Takes 35 minutes to prepare,
  20 minutes to cook

❄

4 x 350 g (12 oz) squash

150 g (5½ oz) dried quinoa

calorie controlled cooking
  spray

2 garlic cloves, crushed

150 g (5½ oz) mushrooms,
  sliced

¼ lemon

150 g (5½ oz) cottage cheese
  with onion and chives

1 tablespoon capers, drained
  and rinsed

a small bunch of fresh parsley
  or basil, chopped

salt and freshly ground black
  pepper

For the sauce

2 garlic cloves, crushed

1 onion, chopped finely

400 g jar passata or 400 g can
  chopped tomatoes

grated zest of an orange

A delicious filling for small squash makes a real treat.

1 Preheat the oven to Gas Mark 5/190°C/fan oven 170°C.
Place the squash on a baking tray and pierce in several places
with the tip of a knife. Bake for 30 minutes or until tender.
Remove from the oven and leave until cool enough to handle.

2 Meanwhile, put the quinoa in a saucepan with double the
amount of water. Bring to the boil and simmer for 15 minutes
or until tender. Drain and place in a large bowl.

3 Heat a large non stick frying pan and spray with the cooking
spray. Stir-fry the garlic for a minute, add the mushrooms
and stir-fry on a high heat for 3–4 minutes or until softened.
Squeeze over the lemon, season and add to the bowl with the
cooked quinoa.

4 Slice the top off each squash, put to one side and then scoop
out the seeds from the squash and discard them. Scoop out
some of the flesh from each, leaving enough for the squash to
retain their shape. Chop the flesh and add to the quinoa and
mushroom mixture. Stir the cottage cheese, capers and parsley
or basil into the quinoa and mushroom mixture.

5 Place the squashes in an ovenproof dish and spoon the
quinoa mixture into the centre of each. Bake for 20 minutes.

6 Meanwhile, make the sauce. Spray the non stick frying pan
again and stir-fry the garlic and onion for a few minutes or until
the onion is soft. Add the passata or tomatoes and orange zest
and simmer for 10 minutes or until thick. Season to taste and
serve with the squash.

Summer lemon spaghetti

Serves 2
385 calories per serving
Takes 20 minutes

❄

175 g (6 oz) dried spaghetti
225 g (8 oz) frozen broad
  beans
a kettleful of boiling water
calorie controlled cooking
  spray
1 garlic clove, crushed
finely grated zest of a lemon
1 tablespoon lemon juice
2 tablespoons chopped fresh
  flat leaf parsley
salt and freshly ground black
  pepper

*A simple, light and refreshing dish with a subtle hint
of lemon.*

1 Bring a pan of water to the boil, add the pasta and cook for
about 8–10 minutes, or according to the packet instructions,
until tender.

2 Meanwhile, place the broad beans in a bowl, pour over the
boiling water, leave to stand for 5 minutes and then drain.
Remove the beans from their skins and discard the skins.

3 Spray a non stick frying pan with the cooking spray. Add
the garlic and cook for 30 seconds. Add the lemon zest, lemon
juice, broad beans and seasoning and stir-fry for 2–3 minutes.

4 Drain the spaghetti and mix it into the frying pan with the
parsley. Serve warm.

Chargrilled vegetable tabbouleh

Serves 2
189 calories per serving
Takes 35 minutes

60 g (2 oz) dried bulgur wheat

300 ml (10 fl oz) vegetable stock

1 red pepper, de-seeded and cut into pieces

3 baby courgettes, halved lengthways

2 baby leeks, halved lengthways

3 baby aubergines, halved

calorie controlled cooking spray

juice of a lemon

1 tablespoon finely chopped fresh mint

1 tablespoon finely chopped fresh coriander

1 tablespoon finely chopped fresh flat leaf parsley

salt and freshly ground black pepper

4 tablespoons 0% fat Greek yogurt, to serve

Baby vegetables are a great addition to this salad, but if you can't find them then use regular size aubergine, leeks and courgettes and cut them into small pieces.

1 Put the bulgur wheat and vegetable stock into a saucepan and bring to the boil. Simmer for 10–15 minutes until tender. Season generously with black pepper and set aside.

2 Meanwhile, heat a griddle pan or non stick frying pan until hot and spray the pepper, courgettes, leeks, and aubergines with the cooking spray. In batches, cook the vegetables in the pan for 8–10 minutes, until charred and cooked. Transfer each batch to a large salad bowl and cover with cling film.

3 Drain the bulgur wheat and stir it into the cooked vegetables. Squeeze over the lemon juice, toss through the herbs and season. Serve immediately, topped with 2 tablespoons of the Greek yogurt each.

Delicious desserts

Summer fruit profiteroles

Serves 6

197 calories per serving

Takes 20 minutes to prepare + cooling, 25 minutes to cook

For the profiteroles

75 g (2¾ oz) plain white flour
60 g (2 oz) low fat spread
2 eggs, beaten

For the sauce

250 g (9 oz) frozen summer fruits, defrosted
1½ tablespoons artificial sweetener

For the filling

250 g (9 oz) Quark
1 teaspoon vanilla extract
2 tablespoons artificial sweetener

With a delicious creamy filling, these are a wonderful treat.

1 Preheat the oven to Gas Mark 6/200°C/fan oven 180°C.

2 Sift the flour on to a piece of greaseproof paper that has been folded in half and then opened out again.

3 Place the low fat spread in a non stick saucepan with 150 ml (5 fl oz) of cold water and bring to the boil. Remove from the heat and tip in the flour, stirring with a wooden spoon until the mixture comes together in a smooth ball. Sit the pan in a basin of cold water until the dough is cool.

4 Gradually beat in the eggs, until you have a smooth batter that drops easily from the spoon. Scatter droplets of water over two baking trays and then place 9 heaped teaspoonfuls of the batter on to each tray, leaving room for the profiteroles to rise.

5 Bake for 18–20 minutes until the profiteroles are well risen and quite brown. Turn off the oven, make a small hole in each profiterole to release the steam and return to the oven for a further 5 minutes to crisp up. Cool on a wire rack.

6 For the sauce, blend the summer fruits to a purée in a food processor or blender and then pass through a sieve to remove any pips and seeds. Stir in the sweetener.

7 For the filling, mix the Quark, vanilla extract and sweetener together. Split the profiteroles open and stuff each one with a teaspoon of filling. Serve three profiteroles per person, with the sauce poured over the top.

Tip... Don't fill the profiteroles too far in advance (30 minutes at the most) as they will start to go soft.

Mango fool

Serves 4
150 calories per serving
Takes 5 minutes

2 ripe mangos
100 g (3½ oz) low fat crème fraîche
90 g (3¼ oz) low fat natural yogurt
8 wafer thin biscuits, to serve

A creamy and fruity dessert.

1 Peel the mangos and cut off the flesh from the stone. Place half the fruit in a food processor and blend until smooth. Chop the remaining fruit and divide between four ramekins or glasses, reserving some for decoration.

2 Beat together the crème fraîche and yogurt and stir in the puréed mango.

3 Pour the creamy mango mixture over the chopped mango and top with the reserved fruit. Chill until ready to serve. Serve with the wafer thin biscuits, for dipping.

Fig and raspberry clafoutis

Serves 6

134 calories per serving

Takes 10 minutes to prepare +
20 minutes resting,
30–35 minutes to cook

calorie controlled cooking
spray

125 g (4½ oz) raspberries

**4 fresh figs, trimmed and
quartered**

2 eggs

50 g (1¾ oz) caster sugar

50 g (1¾ oz) plain white flour

425 ml (15 fl oz) skimmed milk

1 teaspoon vanilla extract

**½ teaspoon icing sugar, for
dusting**

*A clafoutis is a French recipe for a light and sweet batter
pudding. Traditionally made with prunes, this fresh fruit
version uses raspberries and figs instead.*

1 Preheat the oven to Gas Mark 5/190°C/fan oven 170°C
and place a baking tray in the oven to preheat. Lightly spray a
23 cm (9 inch) ovenproof baking dish with the cooking spray
and scatter in the raspberries and figs.

2 Whisk the eggs and sugar together in a large mixing bowl
for about 3 minutes until pale, frothy and roughly doubled in
volume. Sift in the flour and beat until smooth. Whisk in the
milk and vanilla extract and pour the batter over the fruit in
the dish.

3 Bake on the preheated baking tray for 30–35 minutes until
puffy and golden. Leave to rest for 20 minutes, as the pudding
is better served warm rather than hot. Dust with the icing sugar
just before serving.

Variation... Try making a storecupboard version of this
recipe by replacing the fresh figs and raspberries with a
411 g can of apricot halves in natural juice, drained and
patted dry on kitchen towel.

Amaretti honeyed ice cream

Serves 6

137 calories per serving

Takes 10 minutes to prepare
+ freezing

500 g tub reduced fat
ready-made custard

2 tablespoons clear honey

50 g (1¾ oz) amaretti biscuits,
crushed roughly

6 fan wafers, to serve

This home-made ice cream is easy to make and yet impressive. Serve it in pretty glass dishes.

1 Mix all the ingredients together and pour into a shallow, lidded, freezerproof container. Freeze for an hour and then stir well to break up the crystals that have formed around the edges.

2 Return to the freezer and repeat every hour for the next 3 hours until smooth. Alternatively, you could churn it in an ice cream machine.

3 Serve two scoops each with a wafer.

Variations... Affogato is ice cream served in hot espresso coffee. To make it, pour espresso coffee into a shallow cup or glass and add a scoop of the ice cream.

For a tutti frutti version, add 60 g (2 oz) mixed dried fruit, such as raisins, sultanas, chopped glacé cherries and chopped candied peel, soaked in 3 tablespoons of orange juice for 20 minutes, instead of the biscuits.

Pears in mulled wine

Serves 4

225 calories per serving

Takes 10 minutes to prepare,
15–20 minutes to cook

4 pears (not too ripe)

300 ml (10 fl oz) cranberry
juice

300 ml (10 fl oz) red wine

1 cinnamon stick

6 cloves

2 star anise (optional)

50 g (1¾ oz) light or dark
muscovado sugar

4 tablespoons low fat soft
cheese

4 kumquats or 1 clementine,
sliced

*This pretty dessert is ideal for a festive celebration and
would make an excellent alternative to Christmas pudding
or trifle.*

1 Peel the pears but keep the stalks on. Cut a tiny slice from
the base of each pear to enable them to stand upright.

2 Stand the pears in a saucepan and add the cranberry juice,
red wine, cinnamon stick, cloves, star anise, if using, and most
of the sugar, reserving 4 teaspoons for later. Heat gently until
simmering and then cook gently for about 15–20 minutes, or
until the pears are tender.

3 Cool slightly, slice the pears in half and remove their cores
with a melon baller or sharp knife.

4 Mix together the soft cheese with 2 teaspoons of the
reserved sugar. Spoon into the pears and arrange on serving
plates.

5 Sprinkle the remaining sugar on top of the pears, spoon
some of the red wine liquid on to the plates and decorate with
the kumquats or clementine slices.

Variation... If you don't have the individual spices in your
store cupboard, use 1 teaspoon of ground mixed spice
instead.

Cream hearts with passion fruit

Serves 2
98 calories per serving
Takes 15 minutes + chilling

100 g (3½ oz) natural cottage cheese
50 g (1¾ oz) low fat soft cheese
50 g (1¾ oz) low fat natural yogurt
½ tablespoon artificial sweetener
¼ teaspoon vanilla essence
3 passion fruits
juice of ½ an orange

This recipes uses two heart-shaped 'coeur a la crème' moulds. These moulds have small holes in their base to allow liquid to drain out.

1 Line two 'coeur a la crème' moulds with small squares of muslin or clean thin cloth.

2 Smooth the cottage cheese by pushing it through a sieve with a metal spoon into a large bowl.

3 Add the soft cheese, yogurt, sweetener and vanilla essence. Beat with a hand whisk for a minute or so. Spoon the mixture into your moulds and leave on a cooling rack over a plate in the fridge overnight. Some of the liquid will drain out of the cheese mixture and the hearts will 'set'. Pour away any liquid.

4 To make the sauce, scoop out the seeds and pulp from the passion fruits and stir in the orange juice.

5 Just before eating, place a plate on top of a mould and turn both over together. Gently lift off the mould, then the cloth from the cheese shape. Repeat with the second mould. Drizzle the sauce around the cream hearts and serve.

Tips... The cream hearts are not easy to move once turned out, so position your plate on the mould before turning it over.

If you don't have moulds, you can line a colander or sieve with muslin. This way you will make one larger dome-shaped dessert rather than two heart-shaped ones – it will taste just as good.

Pavlova with roasted vanilla plums

Serves 8

192 calories per serving

Takes 15 minutes to prepare + chilling, 1 hour to cook

For the meringue
3 egg whites
175 g (6 oz) caster sugar

For the filling
750 g (1 lb 10 oz) plums, halved and stoned
3 tablespoons light brown soft sugar
1 vanilla pod, slit lengthways

To serve
150 ml (5 fl oz) low fat whipping cream such as Elmlea
150 g (5½ oz) 0% fat Greek yogurt

Plums and a little spice make this a great autumn or winter pudding.

1 Preheat the oven to Gas Mark 2/150°C/fan oven 130°C. Line a baking tray with non stick baking parchment.

2 In a clean, grease-free bowl, whisk the egg whites until stiff peaks form. Whisk in half the caster sugar until the mixture is thick and glossy and then carefully fold in the remainder. Spread the mixture on to the baking parchment to form a circle approximately 20 cm (8 inch) in diameter and make a slight dip in the middle to hold the filling. Bake for 1 hour until the meringue feels dry and then remove from the oven and, keeping it on the paper, cool on a wire rack.

3 Meanwhile, place the plums in an ovenproof dish, sprinkle over the sugar and drizzle with 150 ml (5 fl oz) of water. Tuck the vanilla pod under the plums. Bake at the same temperature as the meringue for 1 hour until soft and juicy.

4 Take out the vanilla pod and scrape out the seeds. Discard the pod and stir the seeds into the plum juices. Cool and then chill.

5 To serve, slide the meringue on to a plate. Whip the cream until it holds soft peaks and then fold in the yogurt. Spoon the mixture on to the meringue, top with the plums and drizzle over the sauce.

Lemon and blueberry charlottes

Serves 4
138 calories per serving
Takes 10 minutes

10 sponge fingers
grated zest and juice of ½ a lemon
100 g (3½ oz) low fat soft cheese
135 g pot low fat custard
100 g (3½ oz) blueberries
1 teaspoon caster sugar, for dusting

A deliciously creamy dessert that's perfect for serving to friends as it looks so special.

1 Cut each sponge finger lengthways and then in half to make four short pieces. Mix 1 tablespoon of lemon juice with 1 tablespoon of water and brush this all over the sponge fingers. Arrange ten pieces of sponge finger upright around the sides of four ramekins.

2 Whisk the rest of the lemon juice and the lemon zest into the soft cheese and custard and then fold in half of the blueberries. Spoon into the ramekins, inside the lining of sponge fingers.

3 Garnish with the reserved blueberries, a little extra lemon zest and a sprinkling of caster sugar. Serve immediately or cover and chill until ready to serve.

Grape cheesecakes

Serves 4
205 calories per serving
Takes 15 minutes +
  15 minutes chilling + cooling

4 light, crisp biscuits, crushed
**225 g (8 oz) seedless red
  grapes, halved**
**225 g (8 oz) seedless green
  grapes, halved**
**200 g (7 oz) low fat soft
  cheese**
2 teaspoons lemon juice
8 teaspoons demerara sugar

*You'll love these delicious desserts. They have a fantastic
flavour, ideal for rounding off any meal.*

1 Sprinkle the crushed biscuits into four individual heatproof
dishes. Add the red and green grapes.

2 Mix the soft cheese and lemon juice together. Spoon over the
fruit, levelling the surface and then chill for about 15 minutes.
Preheat the grill to medium high.

3 Sprinkle 2 teaspoons of sugar over the surface of each
dessert and place under the grill for about 2 minutes until
bubbling and golden brown. Cool slightly and then serve.
Alternatively, chill before serving.

Tip... Be sure to keep an eye on the desserts as they are
grilled to make sure that they do not burn.

Peach and blueberry brûlée

Serves 2

190 calories per serving

Takes 20 minutes + 2 hours
chilling

1 ripe peach, peeled, stoned
and sliced

125 g (4½ oz) blueberries

150 g (5½ oz) 0% fat Greek
yogurt

100 g (3½ oz) virtually fat free
plain fromage frais

2 tablespoons demerara sugar

*Break into the sweet, crunchy topping to find the creamy,
fruity layer underneath.*

1 Preheat the grill to high. Divide the peach slices between
two ramekin dishes. Scatter the blueberries over the top.

2 Beat together the yogurt and fromage frais and spread
this evenly over the fruit. Sprinkle 1 tablespoon of sugar on the
top of each dish. Place the dishes under the hot grill for about
2 minutes, until the sugar melts and bubbles.

3 Cool and then chill in the fridge for 2 hours, so the sugar
topping forms a crunchy layer.

Tip... It is important that you grill the brûlées under a very
hot grill. If the grill is not hot enough, you'll find that the
yogurt mixture will melt before the sugar caramelises.

Montezuma ice cream with marshmallows

Serves 6

175 calories per serving

Takes 10 minutes + freezing

❄

2 x 22 g sachets low fat
   instant dark hot chocolate

4 tablespoons boiling water

500 g (1 lb 2 oz) 0% fat Greek
   yogurt

50 g (1¾ oz) plain chocolate
   (minimum 70% cocoa
   solids), melted

a pinch of allspice

a pinch of ground ginger

1 tablespoon clear honey

100 g (3½ oz) mini
   marshmallows

*Montezuma was an Aztec king who was reputed to have
drunk vast quantities of a rich, dark, spiced hot chocolate
every day.*

1 In a large bowl, mix the instant hot chocolate to a paste
with the boiling water. Add all the other ingredients except the
marshmallows and blend until smooth and evenly mixed. Fold
in the marshmallows and then tip the mixture into a lidded
freezerproof container. Freeze for an hour and then stir well to
break up the crystals that have formed around the edges.

2 Return to the freezer and repeat every hour for the next
3 hours until smooth. Alternatively, you could churn it in an ice
cream machine.

3 Remove the ice cream from the freezer 30 minutes before
you want to serve it, to allow it to soften.

Tip... If you enjoy your chocolate hit, look for high cocoa
content chocolate (70% or more) in your cooking. This way
you'll still get the same strong chocolate taste, but you use
less.

Raspberry soufflé mousse

Serves 2
96 calories per serving
Takes 20 minutes + 2 hours
chilling

**110 g (4 oz) fresh or frozen
and defrosted raspberries**
½ x 11 g sachet gelatine
**150 g (5½ oz) low fat
raspberry yogurt**
artificial sweetener, to taste
2 egg whites

There is no need to worry about soufflés failing to rise with these easy desserts.

1 Make a collar with non stick baking parchment to go around the outside of two 150 ml (5 fl oz) ramekins. Secure with a paper clip or sticking tape.

2 Set aside a few raspberries for decoration. Push the remaining raspberries through a sieve using the back of a spoon. Discard the pips.

3 Dissolve the gelatine according to the packet instructions using 2 tablespoons of water and then stir into the raspberry purée with the yogurt. Sweeten to taste with the sweetener.

4 In a clean, grease-free bowl, whisk the egg whites until stiff peaks form. Stir 1 tablespoon of the whites into the raspberry mixture to slacken it and then carefully fold in the remaining whites.

5 Spoon into the prepared ramekins and leave to set in the fridge for at least 2 hours.

6 To serve, carefully remove the collars and decorate the soufflés with the reserved raspberries.

Apricot and banana meringue

Serves 4

140 calories per serving

Takes 35 minutes + cooling

Ⓥ

450 g (1 lb) apricots, halved and stoned
1 tablespoon cornflour
artificial sweetener, to taste
1 banana
2 eggs, separated
1 tablespoon caster sugar

This scrumptious dessert is easy to prepare and tastes delicious.

1 Preheat the oven to Gas Mark 4/180°C/fan oven 160°C.

2 Place the apricots in a pan with 200 ml (7 fl oz) of water and simmer for about 10 minutes until soft and pulpy. Blend the cornflour to a paste with a little water.

3 Remove the apricots from the heat, stir in the blended cornflour and then cook gently for about 2 minutes until the mixture has thickened. Add artificial sweetener to taste and cool slightly.

4 Slice the banana and stir it into the apricots with the egg yolks. Transfer the mixture to an ovenproof dish.

5 In a clean, grease-free bowl, whisk the egg whites until stiff peaks form. Add the sugar and whisk again until stiff and glossy. Pile the meringue on top of the fruit mixture and bake for about 10 minutes until the meringue is golden. Serve warm.

Strawberry and banana crêpes

Serves 4
194 calories per serving
Takes 15 minutes

50 g (1¾ oz) plain white flour
a pinch of salt
1 egg, beaten
125 ml (4 fl oz) skimmed milk
grated zest and juice of ½ an orange
calorie controlled cooking spray
75 g (2¾ oz) reduced sugar strawberry jam
300 g (10½ oz) strawberries, quartered
2 small bananas, sliced
4 tablespoons virtually fat free plain fromage frais, to serve

Pancakes are not just for pancake day – these are wonderful during summer when strawberries are fresh and in season.

1 In a mixing bowl, sift together the flour and salt. Whisk in the egg, followed by the milk, to give a smooth batter. Stir in the orange zest.

2 Preheat a non stick frying pan. Spray with the cooking spray and swirl in one quarter of the pancake batter to coat the base of the pan. Cook for 1–2 minutes, turning halfway, until golden. Remove to a plate and keep warm while you repeat with the remaining batter to make three more pancakes, spraying the pan each time.

3 Meanwhile, in a separate non stick saucepan, gently heat the jam with 2 tablespoons of the orange juice to make a sauce.

4 In a bowl, mix the strawberries and sliced bananas together with the remaining orange juice.

5 To serve, fill each pancake with a quarter of the fruit mixture and then fold in half. Drizzle the strawberry sauce over the pancakes and top with a spoonful of fromage frais.

Index

Other titles in the Weight Watchers Mini Series

ISBN 978-0-85720-932-0

ISBN 978-0-85720-935-1

ISBN 978-0-85720-934-4

ISBN 978-0-85720-938-2

ISBN 978-0-85720-931-3

ISBN 978-0-85720-937-5

ISBN 978-0-85720-936-8

ISBN 978-0-85720-933-7

ISBN 978-1-47111-084-9

ISBN 978-1-47111-089-4

ISBN 978-1-47111-091-7

ISBN 978-1-47111-087-0

ISBN 978-1-47111-090-0

ISBN 978-1-47111-085-6

ISBN 978-1-47111-088-7

ISBN 978-1-47111-086-3

For more details please visit www.simonandschuster.co.uk